W9-CMG-120

RUN FOR IT

A WOMAN'S GUIDE TO RUNNING

RUN FOR IT

FOR EMOTIONAL AND PHYSICAL HEALTH

KAREN BRIDSON

Burford Books

Copyright © 2002 by Karen Bridson

All Rights Reserved. No part of this book may be reproduced
in any manner without the express written consent of the publisher,
except in cases of brief excerpts in critical reviews and articles.
All inquiries should be addressed to: Burford Books, Inc.,
PO Box 388, Short Hills, NJ 07078.

Printed in Canada.

10 9 8 7 6 5 4 3 2 1

Drawings by Sarah Burford

Library of Congress Cataloging-in-Publication Data

Bridson, Karen.
Run for it: a woman's guide to running for physical and emotional health / Bridson, Karen.
p. cm.
Includes bibliographical references (p.).
ISBN 1-58080-100-5 (pbk.)
1. Running for women. I. Title
GV1061.18.W66 B75 2002
796.42'082—dc21

2002002172

For my husband, Bob,

who asked me what I was waiting for.

ACKNOWLEDGMENTS

I'd like to thank a number of people who helped to make this book a reality.

Thanks must first be given to Judy Mahle Lutter, president and cofounder of the Melpomene Institute, for taking the time to answer my many questions on women and running. Her expertise, research, and insight were invaluable. Thank you also to the staff at the Melpomene Institute, who helped dig up essential studies and data for this project.

A big thank-you also goes out to sportsinjury therapist Cheryl Nix, who has taught me virtually everything I know about running injuries. She shared her tips, reviewed some of the text of this book, and worked to help keep me running despite one stubborn injury.

Thanks also to registered dietician Valerie Johnson for her many lessons on nutrition and her help with this book. I would also like to thank Dr. Vivien Fellegi for answering my medical queries (and being a very dedicated student in my half-marathon clinic!).

I would be negligent if I didn't also thank my good friend Gideon Steinberg, triathlete, for being one of my biggest supporters and a fount of running information. Tom Irwin or, as I call him, The Running Encyclopedia, has also been invaluable as both a coach to me and a friend.

I must also thank my mother, Judi, who encouraged me to run my first race and has stood through rain, cold, and hot sun many times since to see me cross that finish line. And to my father, Jim, for taking so much interest and pride in my running career.

CONTENTS

INTRODUCTION

I am a formerly overweight, unhappy woman who completely changed her life with running. At just 19 years old, I was carrying around an extra 30 pounds, had low self-esteem, felt bad about the way I looked, and had crumbling self-confidence. I was about to start university studies and had been warned about the so-called freshman 15, a term referring to the average of 15 pounds students gain in their first year away from home. Another 15 pounds on my frame would have meant I could never shop in a "normal" clothing store. It was a big turning point in my life. So much was about to change already, and I wanted to start this new life in control and feeling better about myself. So I decided to start to run. I began by running on the spot in my bedroom. With tears streaming down my cheeks, I ran and ran as I counted every agonizing minute on the clock radio on the floor at my feet. Six minutes turned into 10 and before I knew it, I was running on the spot for 12 minutes at a time. This was a big deal for me, since I spent much of my time in high school gym class terrorized by the dreaded 12-minute fitness test run. I soon began running back and forth across my bedroom, then graduated to doing laps of my parents' basement. I was too ashamed to let anyone see me running. I felt my body was jiggling all over the place; I thought people would laugh at me. So even after I got to the university, I continued my running sessions behind locked doors in my dorm room. It wasn't long, however, before a friend convinced me to go to the school's track to put my running legs to the test. One lap turned into seven and before you knew it, I was running a few kilometers at a time, albeit with walk breaks. By that following spring, I had run my first 10K race and lost 30 pounds.

I thought it was my weight loss that fueled this unbelievable change in my self-perception. I felt so much better about myself—started walking with a bit of a swagger, even. I thought this had to do only with the fact that it was no longer painful to look at myself naked in the mirror. It took me some time to realize that running had helped me out in many other ways. Logging hundreds of miles and running races made me proud of myself. My runs gave me a chance to sort out my life, take time out for me, and make better choices. While I fell into a depression and developed PMS symptoms after my running career had begun, I believe holding on to my running firmly has been key to my survival through both. Running has become my religion, my therapy, my place of meditation, even an addiction. I need my runs. They are my tools for coping with the world.

While this all may sound crazy, all of the benefits of running I have just outlined have been proven time and time again through extensive scientific study. Running has been used to treat cases of depression, anxiety, and other emotional problems by psychiatrists and psychologists and found to be as effective as medication. Aerobic exercise, like running, is a cornerstone of most PMS treatment programs. Runners tend to have higher self-esteem, more positive body image, less anxiety, and fewer health problems. Not to mention the fact that running is the fastest, most time- and cost-efficient way of losing weight and staying in shape. Few exercises burn calories at this rate (100 calories per 10 minutes) and are as easy to participate in as slipping on your sneakers and running out the door.

The wide-ranging benefits of running are a huge, wonderful secret the running world is sitting on. Almost all the women I've known in my life have suffered from weight problems, body image problems, depression, stress, anxiety, PMS, and the like. When you look at what adding this sport to your life can do for all these problems, I don't know why everyone isn't doing it. Every time a woman tells me about problems like these, I suggest she start running. I have watched so many women leave the running clinics I teach thinner, happier, more confident, and more in control of their lives. I've had these women run up to me in races, choked up with tears, to tell me how much running has changed their lives. We all know the secret now, and I am desperate to tell others. Running can dramatically improve the quality of life for women, and it's just a shame more of us don't know it.

That's why I decided to write this book. I want to spread the word. This is a book guiding people not only in running, but also in using running to help various emotional health issues they may be confronting. Now, I am not a psychologist, nor an emotional health expert of any sort. I am just a woman who has spent a large portion of her life struggling with some of these issues and spent many an hour at kitchen tables talking to other women about their problems. I am also a woman who took control of her life with running, and I want to share the key to this with you. With three marathons now under my belt, and having taught a number of running clinics, I am qualified to walk you through your venture into running. If you are suffering from any kind of emotional trouble, however, it is critical that you be under the care of a medical professional. Running is not a cure-all, simply a tool to help.

My goal in this book is to first convince you that running can indeed change your life. I will do this by bombarding you with the clinical data that supports my claims, and with personal anecdotes. Then I will take you step by step through everything you'll need to know about running. Whether you are just getting started running or have been at it for a while, this book will give you valuable information and pointers that will help you make running a healthy part of your life for your whole life.

PART I

WHY RUN?

CHAPTER ONE

Running, Self-Esteem, and Self-Image

"Self-esteem isn't everything;

it's just there's nothing without it."

—Gloria Steinem, *Revolution from Within*

I am hard-pressed to think of a single woman I've known who hasn't struggled with poor self-esteem and/or a negative body image at some point in her life. Too many of us think we are not pretty enough, not intelligent enough, not thin enough, not busty enough, not charming enough, untalented. This diminished self-concept, both physical and mental, is a pervasive problem for women throughout North America. According to a 1993 national survey of women's health, one in five women has low self-esteem, while a 1996 survey found that 56 percent of women disliked their overall appearance. Meanwhile, a particularly alarming finding came out of a 1984 Melpomene Institute study, which asked physically active women, whose average age was 32, to look at five sketches of body types and pick which one they most wanted to look like. Thirty-eight percent picked the figure that was 20 percent *underweight*, 44 percent picked the figure that was 10 percent underweight, and just 14 percent wanted to be the body size that is considered medically advisable. (See figures below.) Perhaps the results of a 1987 *Ms.* magazine survey sum up the impact of our North American obsession with being thin and its impact on the self-concept of women. The survey found that 64.4 percent of respondents agreed with the sentence, "I would like myself more if I was thinner."

In a society where a woman's value and power are inextricably tied with what she looks like, poor body image and poor self-esteem often go hand in hand, one feeding the other.

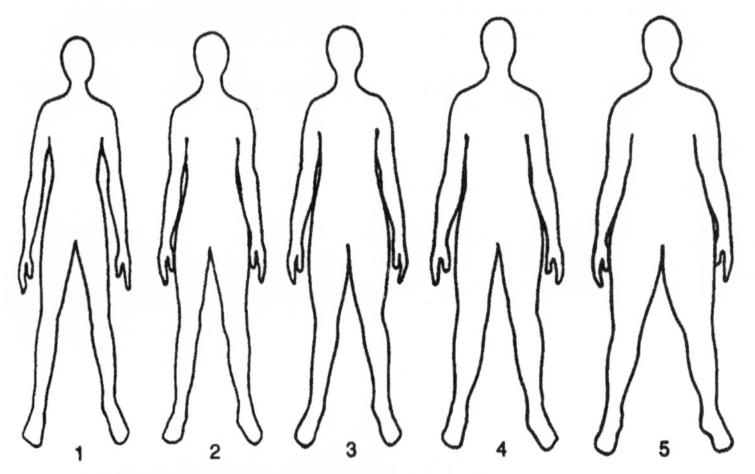

These drawings represent body types that are (1) 20 percent underweight, (2) 10 percent underweight, (3) of average weight, (4) 10 percent overweight, and (5) 20 percent overweight. GRAPHIC FROM *THE BODYWISE WOMAN*, COURTESY OF THE MELPOMENE INSTITUTE. www.melpomene.org and health@melpomene.org

Both our self-esteem and body image begin to develop in childhood, when we first look to others to get a sense of who we are and how we fit into the world around us. Unfortunately, many children, particularly girls, are bombarded early in life by negative feedback and images that result in their thinking less of themselves than they should. Everything from being told you were fat as a child, to being abused, to seeing idealized images of anorexic models in magazines can contribute to the development of poor self-esteem and body image. The pictures we carry inside our minds of our physical and internal selves are often not based in, and are far more negative than, reality. It doesn't help that we live in a society where the current ideal of beauty is "the thinner, the better." Today's so-called supermodels weigh on average 23 percent less than the average woman. In the last 20 years, the *Playboy* centerfold has lost 25 pounds and is 18 percent thinner than what is considered to be the medical ideal or normal for her age and height. Try as we may, many women have a hard time escaping the pressures that come with these societal ideals. And again, with our power in this world tied to our physicality, our self-esteem is greatly impacted by these images.

Having poor self-esteem and poor body image ultimately means we do not think we are as beautiful, smart, talented, capable, and deserving as we truly are. We may turn away from or miss out on opportunities, both personal and professional, allow ourselves to be treated poorly, and lead a life that is less fulfilling than it could be. We may feel ashamed of our bodies, feel guilty about eating, and hide behind baggy clothing, makeup, our children, or other shields. The bottom line: We underestimate our power and value and will likely be unhappy as a result. Sadly, many of us know this about ourselves, but don't know what to do, or where to start, to change it.

While overcoming poor self-esteem and body image is a complex struggle, running can be one way of speeding that process. Running can help improve your self-concept in a number of ways. First, adding a running regime to your life will no doubt result in weight loss, strength gain, and improved overall health. As a result, you will feel better physically, feel a sense of accomplishment, and feel a level of control over your life and body that you may not have experienced before. You may also find you come out of it with a sense of pride in yourself and empowerment after having set a goal and achieved it. And as we will see in other chapters, running helps clear away depression, anxiety, stress, and other emotional barriers that have stood in the way of your having a clear and accurate self-portrait. When you are calm and happy, you are better equipped to take a good look at you. All these factors come together to make you feel better about your body, feel more self-confident, and ultimately enjoy improved self-esteem and body image.

RUNNING CHANGED MY SELF-CONCEPT

Here's a story that exemplifies the impact running has had on my self-esteem and sense of my physical self. It's the tale of my relationship with makeup. When I was 18 years old, I was physically incapable of leaving my house without cosmetics on. The thought of venturing out sans makeup was horrifying. I didn't believe I was beautiful without it. I would cover myself up with loose black clothing, cake on the makeup, and do my hair up like I was heading to a music video shoot (albeit, it was the 1980s!). I just didn't have the self-confidence to be my natural self in public. In fact, my friends once tried to get me to go out without makeup and I simply couldn't do it. Ten years later I am proud to say I can, and often do, stand around in very public places completely au naturel, covered in sweat, in unflattering little outfits, all the while being absolutely proud of myself and filled with confidence. The first time I realized the change in me was after one of my races. I was basking in the glory of what I had just achieved when it occurred to me that I was strutting and I didn't have a stitch of makeup on. I was a strong, able, healthy woman who had just done something great and I didn't need to hide behind anything.

This tale is about more than makeup. I wore makeup all the time because I didn't feel good enough without it. Running has in so many ways helped me find my self-confidence. My self-esteem and self-image have blossomed since I started running. This change began with my weight loss. As my body got smaller, and healthier, I slowly began to feel more secure about how I looked. Once I reached my ideal weight, I noticed I had less anxiety about walking across a room in front of people, I could get up off the floor easier, and people treated me differently (a sad, but true fact).

But this change in me runs deeper than just the superficial. I am proud of the miles I have run. I am proud of the fact that I said I was going to start running, I did it, and I didn't stop. I never in a million years would have thought I'd run three marathons. But even before I started running longer races, I was enormously proud of what I had accomplished with my running. How can you not feel good about yourself when you're out there pounding the pavement? You could be at home sitting on the couch, dry and comfy, but you're not, you're out there doing it. You've become someone who does it, not just talks about it. Once you've run three minutes without stopping, a mile, a 5K—whatever it is that you never thought you'd be able to do—something in you changes. It's a real high. I've seen women in my running clinics laughing, smiling, and jumping for joy each time they do something that had once been beyond their comprehension. And as you continue to do more and more, you begin to realize that you can do whatever you set your mind to. It's empowering.

Judy Mahle Lutter is cofounder and president of the Melpomene Institute for women, an organization devoted to women's health and activity. Her organization's studies have shown that women find exercise helps them look at their bodies in a different way. "A lot of women indicated that being physically active gave them a way to focus on the strength and power of their bodies and less on the way their bodies looked," she says. "It becomes more about what your body can do. We're trying to get women to look at their bodies in a more holistic way." When you run, you feel strong. And that spills over to every part of your life.

RUNNING'S IMPACT ON SELF-CONCEPT: WHAT SCIENCE TELLS US

I have met hundreds of women over the years whose self-concept has been dramatically improved since they took up running. But proof of running's impact on self-esteem and body image goes beyond tales of personal experience. There's a great deal of scientific research showing that runners and those participating in other regular aerobic pursuits notice marked improvements in their self-image, body image, and self-esteem. A number of studies conducted throughout the 1970s showed that exercise training increases emotional stability, self-confidence, conscientiousness, self-sufficiency, and persistence. Scientists at Indiana's Purdue University reported in 1973 that high-fitness adults had greater emotional stability, imaginativeness, and self-sufficiency than did adults with low levels of fitness. And in a study published in the *Journal of Sports Medicine and Fitness* in 1967, scientists found that those who exercised regularly for four or more years showed greater ambition and optimism than a group just starting an exercise program. In 1990 the Melpomene Institute for Women's Health Research in St. Paul, Minnesota, surveyed 600 women about why they exercise. Seventeen percent said it helped them realize a positive self-image, not just because of the weight control effects, but because of the fitness, endurance, and strength gained.

Runners have also been found to be low on anxiety and high on self-esteem and to have either possessed or developed high levels of self-sufficiency and imagination. It also appears these benefits increase with the amount of exercise. With all this evidence, it's a wonder to me why more women don't run. It's as though the benefits of running are the running community's best-kept secret.

TAKE CONTROL

With all of this said, I must add that for most women, body image and self-esteem will be issues they struggle with their entire lives. Running can make that journey a whole lot easier, that's all. Today I weigh 145 pounds, which is smack dab in the middle of my ideal BMI and in the perfect range on all other weight charts. I remain concerned about my weight, however, and I believe I always will be. I often think I should be thinner for all of the running I do. Despite the four-month training schedules I follow for marathon training regularly, my body refuses to budge more than 5 pounds in any direction. Another woman doing the amount of running I do would have to eat a bunch more for fear of withering away. You see, everyone's metabolism is different. My body tends to be overweight; I must run consistently to keep it in a healthy range. Meanwhile, my husband can go months without exercising without much muscle tone loss or weight gain. It's all about what is healthy and attainable for you. Once you've reached that, your body will let you know by seemingly wanting to stay within a certain range.

As with all women, my level of self-esteem is subject to the day. Sometimes I am pretty hard on myself; other days I think I'm okay. And running has been a big part of my being able to maintain an improved sense of myself on both the physical and emotional fronts. Running is not a cure-all and it won't help you feel better about yourself overnight. But it can be an important part of getting you on that journey.

MEG'S STORY: ON SELF-IMAGE

Meg Devine, 24, Rochester, New York

Until she entered college, Meg Devine had always had a healthy body weight and been relatively active. But when she went off to school, she lost any semblance of a healthy perspective on her body. Her self-esteem began to plummet, leading to depression and bouts with an eating disorder. Her discovery of running, and its emotional and physical health benefits, helped her regain control of her body and mind. Ultimately, Meg says, running helped her rediscover balance and what she calls " a comfort zone." Here's her story:

All my life I've been sort of a normal-sized person—not too big and not too small, so to speak. I've always been active. I played soccer and lacrosse in high school, danced, and did other things a girl should do growing up. College hit, though, and suddenly that wasn't quite enough. "Normal-sized" felt big and ungainly, and for one reason or another, I started sliding down a spiral of negativity. Whether it was being away from home, the stress of academics, or fighting to maintain a peer group, I began to feel isolated and depressed about my self-image. (I guess I figured, "Hey, I can't change any of these other circumstances . . . how about blaming myself?")

I fought for balance for years, trying aerobics (the other perky women in the classes just highlighted what I saw as my own fatal flaws), crew (I always ended up feeling like a failure next to the girls whose bodies were naturally more muscular than mine), and other outlets. But my self-image problems had become a pattern. In stressful situations, new environments, fresh relationships, and other places where I felt unsure, I would cling to the one thing I could take hold of—myself. I developed disordered eating patterns, flirting with anorexia, then plunging into bulimia. It was always a result of depression and second-guessing myself in shaky life situations. Not a good scene—it feeds on itself, thrusting you farther and farther into depression.

Now for the sunny resolution. I discovered running. I was a senior in college when I started to run regularly, not just as a part of another sport. With a friend who also was not a "runner," I started small. Gradually, we built up to nice steady running regimen. I discovered first that running was a superb way to stay fit, but, more importantly, that it let me concentrate on myself. It was time alone to think, to pray, to "find my center," or to think of nothing at all. And it was an accomplishment every time. Every single time I come back from a run, I feel like I've achieved something. It was a step toward health, mental and physical. The change in my attitude, in my self-confidence, in my ability to face difficult situations, in my recognition of who I am and what I want to do in life—it all came into focus a little better.

A good example of how running changed everything was when I moved to New York City after college. Talk about new situations! This small-town girl felt scared, alone, intimidated, and nervous about the big city. I felt the familiar instinct to withdraw, that old need to overcontrol myself. So the first thing I did was to find a place to run. In Central Park, with all the other NYC runners—grandmothers, marathoners, high schoolers, and potbellied middle-aged men—I found my comfort zone. With all those strangers running, but with the chance to focus on myself, I managed to stem the tide of depression and self-questioning before it could grab me.

I won't say that I'm "cured"—I think I'll always have misgivings about myself. But I have a tool now. Running is a trusty inner tool that connects me to my environment instead of closing me off from it. I can run no matter where I am or who I'm with. And I have that knowledge in myself. I know that when my heart gets pumping and I make my legs go for 10 extra minutes, I'll feel triumphant. Even if I don't go the 10 extra, and I just manage to get up out of bed in the morning and jog for half an hour, it's still another day I've done something good for myself. I'm slow, I know, and I may never run a marathon. It doesn't matter—I've done something much better: I've discovered the gift of balance.

SHASTA'S STORY: ON LOVING HERSELF

Shasta Townsend, 27, Toronto, Canada

For Shasta Townsend, running has meant improved emotional health on a number of fronts: improving her body image and self-esteem, giving her an outlet for stress, and helping her see the value of healthy life choices. Here is her story:

Before my body turned into something female—before the times of maxi pads and push-up bras—I was actually quite athletic. During those elementary school days, I was active in track and field, relay running, and long-distance cross-country running. I was on every team and in every sport. Even if I was not the star, I was always in the starring lineup. It was a time in my life I remember fondly and, oddly, the memory of running looms large in those remembrances. I remember early-morning runs across the open fields behind my school, the smell of wild sage and the sounds of meadowlarks. As things seem to turn out with most children moving into adolescence, however, I became more interested in Duran Duran, Maybelline, and a certain boy. Early-morning runs turned into early-morning regrets thanks to late-night parties. The thought of running after a night of lemon gin and anonymous encounters did not appeal to my 16-year-old body and mind. I somehow lost the path for many years but gained significant pounds. Although athletic during elementary school, I have battled with extra pounds my entire life. Adolescence and the birth control pill were not kind. I gained 30 pounds in six months and have just recently—10 years later—lost them. As women, we not only fight unwanted pounds but the feeling of shame associated with our self-perception that we are fat and unattractive. It is a fight I abhor and yet have engaged in. The battle scars are still apparent. I lived on a Diet Coke diet, began smoking, binged, vomited, starved, ate only carrots, ate only soup, ate only fruit, did not eat dessert, did not eat fat, did not eat meat, ate only popcorn, and hated thin people. Seems the more I tried, the worse I felt, physically and mentally.

BACK TO RUNNING: *It was not until my mental state was deteriorating and my stress level skyrocketing thanks to a psychotic boss and poisonous work environment that I began to look at my lifestyle and the choices I was making. This was well into my 20s. Feeling out of control, angry, and frustrated one day, I threw on a pair of old running shoes and hit the trails along the lake. I just knew I needed to vent the anger, frustration, and lack of control I was feeling. And yelling at my partner was not an option. Suddenly, running past the birds bobbing up and down on Lake Ontario into a setting sun brought back a memory of peace and satisfaction that I had not known in years. It was that memory of early-morning runs across Saskatchewan prairies before the time of careers, two-piece suits, and Hitler-esque bosses that suddenly flooded back. That sense of calm, self-assuredness, and self-satisfaction I had searched for years was suddenly returning. From my view across the lake, I gained a perspective I had lost. Somehow sweat and heavy breathing brought it all back. I began running three times a week before work—not far but far enough to find my strength to continue the day. After several months, I was losing weight, gaining muscle and confidence. I felt like a different person and knew it was time to change my life. Shortly after I quit the job that caused me insomnia, shakes, and inexpressible frustration. In the words of many self-help gurus, I made a commitment to myself and my body to promote the positive. That meant early-morning runs after a bottle of red wine and late-evening runs after 12-hour days. It meant a new job and losing some old friends who couldn't get past high school. It's also meant a new wardrobe with small sizes, an increased athleticism and general positive feeling, and a renewed sense of self-worth. It meant looking into the mirror and genuinely liking the person looking back.*

CHAPTER TWO

Combating Stress

"I would like to suggest that running should be reviewed as a wonder drug, analogous to penicillin, morphine and the tricyclics. It has a profound potential in preventing mental and physical disease and in rehabilitation after various diseases have occurred."

—Dr. William Morgan, president of the American Psychological Association's Division of Exercise and Sport Psychology, 1989

Stress is something that affects all of us in some way, to some degree, in almost everything we do. It's hard to get away from. This pressure and tension we call stress is a part of this high-tech, everything-must-be-done-now world most of us live in today. Women who work full time and have children under the age of 13 are the most stressed-out people on the planet, according to a Roper Starch Worldwide survey of 30,000 people between the ages of 13 and 65. That study also showed that globally, 23 percent of professional women felt "super-stressed." Stress contributes to heart disease, high blood pressure, strokes, obesity, and many, many other medical problems. As a result, tranquilizers, antidepressants, and anti-anxiety medications account for one-quarter of all prescriptions written in the United States each year. Aside from its physiological manifestations, stress also impacts our emotional lives, beyond just making us feel frantic and pressured. It can lead to depression, strain our relationships, make us say and do things we later regret, even cause our professional performance to suffer. Fortunately, more and more people today are recognizing the impact stress is having on their personal and professional lives, not to mention their health, and are increasingly turning to medication, therapy, even Eastern healing therapies, in an effort to escape.

RUN FROM YOUR STRESS

Running is one of the greatest ways of escaping from stress temporarily and curbing the negative effects it has on us emotionally, spiritually, and physically. You can literally run away from your stressors. If you've had a particularly hard day at work, you can grab a banana from the snack shop and put on your running shoes the second you get through the door. I guarantee you'll feel like a different person when you get back. After a run, it's impossible to stay as stressed and wound up as you were. The chemical change involved, the physical removal from the stressful situations, the autohypnotic effect, the time to yourself—all of it comes together to help you de-stress yourself.

Science has proven time and again that aerobic exercise can have a significant impact on stress. In fact, many psychologists and psychiatrists prescribe aerobic exercise to people suffering from emotional problems, including stress. A review of multiple studies published in the *Clinical Psychology Review* found that aerobic exercise training has antidepressant and anxiety-relieving effects and protects against the harmful consequences of stress. And a study conducted in 1981 concluded that anxiety levels in both normal and anxious people were reduced after vigorous exercise. Those who exercise regularly also have lower levels of anxiety than nonexercisers. This was seen in a study of 100 males at an American university in 1989, when researchers placed the men into five different jogging groups, from advanced runners to nonrunners. Using a number of anxiety inventories, the researchers found running lessened trait anxiety, hostility, and aggression. Analysis of four population surveys out of the United States and Canada in 1988 also found that a person's level of physical activity was positively associated with general well-being, lower levels of anxiety, and positive mood.

Research has gone so far as to indicate that exercise can be as effective in relaxing people as medication. According to a scientific review published in *Physician and Sportsmedicine* in 1981, a 15-minute walk at a heart rate of 100 beats per minutes has a significantly greater effect on resting muscle tissue than a single dose of tranquilizer. Exercise training can also reduce fatigue while increasing vigor, according to a study of middle-aged healthy adults who were put through a 10-week walking-jogging program. Proving the direct and long-lasting relaxing effect of running, a group of scientists in 1981 studied a group of runners and found they were less stressed by various stimuli after runs—and that the effects were noted as long as five hours later. In 1984 researchers collected data from 278 managers from 12 different corporations at three points over a four-year period. They found that physical activity had a significant buffering effect, allowing people who exercise regularly to be more resistant to the detrimental physiological and psychological effects of stressful life events. This included even some of the most severe stressors, like the loss of a spouse. Runners even exhibit less anxiety about death than do nonrunners.

There are a number of reasons why running has a relaxing effect on us. Most people have heard of the "runner's high" or the improved mood that comes over a person after a certain amount of running time has passed. While researchers are not sure whether the release of brain neurotransmitters is what sparks the improved mood, there's no doubt running results in an elevated sense of well-being. It is also believed that the high may come from a form of autohypnosis, with the first portion of our runs slowly inducing a hypnotic state. Aerobic exercise also increases blood flow, helping relieve tension in the muscles. All of these factors together, perhaps combined with some unknown, effectively work to relax us when we run.

PUT YOUR RUNS TO WORK

When I've had a particularly upsetting event occur, one of the first things I think about is going for a run. I need one. It helps me get rid of that sick feeling in my gut. It gives me a chance to think about things clearly and figure out what my next move will be. Even when nothing in particular is upsetting me, I'll consciously ask myself what is going on in my life that I'm worried or a bit upset about and I'll make the decision to think about this while I'm running. I do this because I know that when I'm done I'll feel better about the situation and I'll come out of it with a game plan. You cannot conjure up that negative emotion you went out onto your run with after you come back. Just try to wipe the smile off your face.

Running also helps me zone out, which helps the run go by painlessly. Some of my best runs have been when I've been quite upset about something. But don't try to run and cry at the same time—it's one fast way to hyperventilate! I found that out the hard way. You need to be able to breathe in a controlled rhythm to run well, something that's not entirely possible when you are crying. Seriously, that's a big part of what makes you feel better, too: breathing. Big deep breaths will calm you down whether you are running or sitting still. Running just happens to force you to do it. They say the calming effect smokers feel they get from cigarettes has more to do with breathing in deeply and holding it—the way they do when they take a drag—than anything to do with the chemicals they are ingesting. (Those chemicals actually make their heart rate go through the roof.)

You make better decisions after a run, you can be more sure of not overreacting, you can put things into better perspective, and you feel more confident that you've done what you need to do to make a good decision. Often the stress we're facing is just a part of our normal lives. There's nothing specific we need to do, just get away from it all for a while. And that's what your runs can give you. As a former crime reporter whose job often involved interviewing the parents of murdered and killed children, I more often than not came home with my shoulders tied in knots from the stress of my day. If it weren't for my runs, I don't know how I would have made it through day after day of dealing with that kind of job. (It must be said, however, that I can't imagine the stress the people I was interviewing were going through.)

Judy Mahle Lutter, of the Melpomene Institute, says that just the fact that you're out on the road alone with other runners can help you de-stress. "One thing that I've found and that is supported by the data is that it seems easier to talk about stressful issues when you're being physically active," she notes. "When you are running with a group of friends it's acceptable and easy to talk about your problems. I think this happens much more frequently on the run than over coffee. It's hard to explain why." Those solitary runs can be equally good at helping you unwind, she adds. "I run every day after work. It's a time when I can sort things through and come up with much better solutions." Lutter says she also encourages women to work up to longer runs. "It seems to me that it takes several miles before I can shake all the stuff that's going on and free up my mind to other things."

YOUR ESCAPE

There's nothing like going for a run when it all feels like too much. It may seem at first like going for a run is just one more thing you have to squeeze into your day, but once you get hooked, you'll see it's the one thing you really do need to do to find clarity in a hectic day. Science has proven that running is a great tool to combat stress. Take advantage of that free, self-directed form of therapy by adding running to your life. You'll be glad you did.

GILLIAN'S STORY: ON STRESS AND RUNNING

Gillian Doran, 35, Chester, England

The decision to start running came to Gillian Doran very suddenly one day. When her husband found himself without a job, this mother of three felt her already high level of stress suddenly become too much. Here's her story:

My husband leaving work was the icing on the cake. I usually can't spend enough time with him, but at that time, I couldn't bear his presence in the house. I was extremely tense, felt suffocated, and literally felt the "fight-or-flight" response; there was a real physical urge to run, which I just went along with. There was an immediate lifting of spirits entirely due to running. I went through a few weeks of feeling like Rocky when he runs up all those steps and dances at the top, hands in salute; I always ran home smiling. It felt really good—a physical release from tension. I was noticeably less tense and aggressive even. My husband was impressed by the change in me and offered encouragement. I was often tired from lack of sleep but found running helped me cope better with that—the exercise gave me more energy. I got more work done and coped better with the kids and daily problems, had more patience and greater clarity of mind. My stressors have evaporated naturally. Many things that were a problem in the beginning have changed. My husband easily found another job, our financial situation changed for the better, and the baby started sleeping through the night (not every night by any means!), so I tend to get more sleep now. But I am sure that the running has helped. Maybe it's having time to myself. There's not much, but it's better than nothing. (I'm lucky to go to the loo on my own, let alone anything else!) Maybe it's to do with my raised confidence levels from doing something so positive for myself and getting positive feedback from others; maybe it's just that I appreciated that I had to cope better with stress and I am undergoing a period of change. If I am feeling stressed, though, a run always, always makes me feel better. I think it's a short-term effect, but I find it helps me to focus my mind on the problem and deal with it in the long run.

ON STICKING WITH IT: *I find now that I have to run farther to get the same physical release, the "Rocky effect." But that's motivation in itself. I am lazy at times, though, and do find it hard to get motivated some days. Even if I go a week without running, I know I can start again and build up speeds and times quickly. I know I'm not a decent runner but I do see that the fat chap who laughed at me when I started doesn't laugh now—and he's still fat, and I'm not. I feel great that I started doing it, and that I've kept it up. I hadn't run for 16 years and have only played badminton and done one term of yoga class plus a few aerobics videos in the interim. Everyone I know has been surprised by me doing it.*

ON FITTING IT ALL IN: *I get a lot of people saying to me that they'd do it too if only they had the time, but what they mean is that it's just not a priority for them. I changed my routine to fit it in—started getting up at 6:15 A.M. to go for a run before my husband left for work. On weekends, if he's home, I can have a lie-in. Running is cheap and doesn't take up much time—a very efficient form of exercise.*

LYDIA'S STORY: ON COPING

Lydia Bruce-Burgess, 24, London, England

Despite being raised in a family of runners, Lydia Bruce-Burgess didn't realize the benefits of running until she started feeling the pressures of school. This Ph.D. student, whose parents founded the New Forest Runners Club in England, began running at the age of three, but says it wasn't until she stopped running for a year that she saw what her life would be like without running. Here's her story:

ON STRESS AND ANXIETY: *Running sorts out my stress. Ever since I was a child I have tended to worry overly about everything. As a teenager I suffered greatly from headaches and migraines; during my A-level [high school] exams I suffered from panic attacks. Running was the only sport that helped me relax. As an adult, I no longer suffer from headaches but during times of stress, like during exams, before deadlines, or before conference presentations, I tend to suffer from eczema, irritable bowel syndrome, and insomnia. Running enables me to relax and put my worries into perspective, which is important because I usually blow my worries out of proportion. At present I am writing my Ph.D., and some of my most innovative ideas for my research have come to me when running! During my master's degrees I stopped running due to work pressures and suffered a great deal more anxiety-related ailments.*

ON FINDING CONFIDENCE: *Aside from feeling good physically and helping me deal with stress, running has also helped me to become a* *more self-confident individual than I think I would have otherwise been. When I first left home to go to university I was fairly shy. I joined my college cross-country team and had so much fun that it really brought me out of my shell. By the final year of my degree, I was the team secretary and had lost all signs of shyness.*

ON PHYSICAL HEALTH: *Running makes me feel better both physically and psychologically. Physically I feel healthy, it reduces the effects of my asthma, lessens period pains, and I get less colds and flu than my nonsporting friends. Also, running has made my body more toned than it would otherwise be. This has helped me feel more confident about my appearance. When I stopped running for a year in 1998–1999, I felt flabby and self-conscious about my body.*

CHAPTER THREE

FIGHTING DEPRESSION

"No depression can stand up to a 10-mile run."

—saying among runners, from *The Exercise Prescription for Depression and Anxiety*

At any given time, there are over 20 million North American adults suffering from depression. In fact, according to the surgeon general of the United States, major depression is the leading cause of disability among developing nations. Meanwhile, women are twice as likely as men to suffer from the disorder, with one in four women likely to experience severe depression in her lifetime. In fact, a survey of women's health conducted in 1993 found that 40 percent of women reported being severely depressed in the past week. While weight control ranked as the number one health concern among women in a study conducted by the Melopomene Institute, emotional and spiritual health ranked second. Our childbearing years are marked by the highest rates of depression, followed by the years prior to menopause. And there is no single face to depression. It can range in severity from significantly diminishing your quality of life to making it impossible to get out of bed. Some cases even end in suicide. In any event, the effects of depression can be devastating. Jeopardizing your relationships, career, finances, and every other facet of your life, depression can make every day emotionally painful.

RUNNING FROM DEPRESSION

So what tools are there to combat this problem? Psychotherapy and drug therapy are the leading treatments for depression, and experts have found they can be very effective. There is something else that can have a dramatically positive impact on depression, however: running.

Before I go on to tell you what scientific study has told us about the benefits of running and how the sport helped me, I must first stress that if you suffer from depression, no matter how severe, you must seek professional help. Reading this book does not qualify. It is essential that you be under the care of a mental health professional. A good place to start is your family doctor. While running was integral to my resurfacing from depression, the therapy I received over the years I was affected deserves equal credit for my recovery. It's not enough to clear your mind, work on your self-esteem, lift your mood, and so on. You must get to the heart of what went wrong to lead you down that road. Therapy is the key to that.

THE BENEFITS

Running's primary weapon against depression is simply its mood-lifting effect. Through chemical changes in your body, running actually changes how you feel. It also helps you relax, zone out, de-stress, let go of tension, feel better about yourself, improve your self-esteem and body image, and much more. All the while, you are in control of making that difference in your life. You are not handing over control or credit for your recovery to a pill or another form of treatment. *You* are doing it. This is not to say that other forms of therapy are not helpful. They definitely can be. But running gives you something you can do every day, at any time, to take control of your mind when you sometimes feel it is in control of you.

HOW RUNNING HELPS

A number of scientific theories have attempted to explain what exactly it is about running that helps depression, anxiety, and the like. No one seems to have the definitive answer, but each of these theories has its merits. It could be that one, none, or all of them are responsible in some way for the emotional benefits of the sport. Keith W. Johnsgard, Ph.D., outlines these theories in his book *The Exercise Prescription for Depression and Anxiety*. One theory suggests that the increased blood flow and oxygenation that occur in our central nervous system while we are running may make us more resilient to environmental stresses. Another thesis says that we may simply be less likely to think of upsetting things while we are running. Some claim that mastering a skill and taking our healing into our own hands are why running helps. But probably the most popular theory on why running helps combat so many emotional problems is biochemical. Proponents of this theory point to the fact that the chemical structure of the beta-endorphin we produce when we run is very similar to that of opium—and 20 to 50 times more potent. Unfortunately, we have not been able to confirm this theory because it is impossible to test what is going on inside the brain of a living person. While it has yet to be proven whether increases in such endorphins cause us to have elated moods, this remains a very popular notion.

PROOF IT WORKS

A great deal of scientific study has been dedicated to looking at whether running and aerobic activity actually have a positive impact on our moods and, specifically, can help treat depression. Time and again, these studies have shown that running can be as effective as or more effective than conventional drug therapies to treat depression.

In a study conducted at Freie University in Berlin in 2001, five men and seven women (with a mean age of 49) walked on a treadmill following an interval-training pattern for 30 minutes for 10 days. At the end of the training program there was a "significant" reduction in depression scores. The researchers concluded that aerobic exercise substantially improves mood in patients with major depressive disorders in a short time. In fact, they found that regular exercise was even more effective than drugs in treating serious depression, because drugs take longer to take effect.

Other studies have found running to be particularly effective adjunct in the treatment of depression and to be at least as effective as, and cheaper than, drug therapy in cases of mild depression. In one study 43 depressed women were randomly assigned to an aerobic exercise regime, a relaxation exercise program, or a group with no treatment. The results showed that those in the aerobic exercise group exhibited greater decreases in depression than those in either of the other groups. Studies have shown that depressive symptoms actually decrease as the levels of physical activity increase. A study conducted in 1988 found that physical inactivity may be a risk factor for depressive symptoms. Running has even been used in the management of people with severe anxieties, including obsessive-compulsive disorder.

One study of 1,000 college students found that treadmill running reduced the severity and duration of depressive symptoms. A random survey found that 72 percent of those who exercised sufficiently to maintain moderate levels of fitness (equivalent to 10K of running or walking a week) claimed that they were "very happy." Among people who answered they were either "pretty happy" or "not so happy," only slightly more than one-third were physically fit. The researchers concluded that there is a significant association between happiness and optimal physical fitness. A recent review of studies on this topic by researchers at the Rex Sports Medicine Institute in Cary, North Carolina, concluded that physical activity plays an important role in the management of mild to moderate mental health diseases, especially depression and anxiety. In fact, the review concluded that increased aerobic exercise can be beneficial to those who suffer from panic disorders.

A PRESCRIPTION FOR GOOD MENTAL HEALTH

Dr. Johnsgard, a marathon runner and psychologist, often prescribes exercise to patients who are suffering from a variety of emotional concerns. "Depression is a major mental health problem in America, and with the exception of the bipolar disorders, exercise appears to be an effective treatment," he says. "Exercise therapy appears to be as powerful as antidepressant drugs and the psychotherapies, and it offers many strengths and advantages which those more conventional treatments do not offer. Its side effects are beneficent and life-enhancing." In his book Dr. Johnsgard outlines a number of case studies in which he prescribed exercise and running to his patients with great success.

MY EXPERIENCE

My major depressive episode hit while I was in the middle of my university career and almost forced me to leave school. It culminated in a halfhearted suicide attempt, followed my an emergency room visit, a stay in a psychiatric ward, and years of therapy. I was never diagnosed with any specific disorder, nor ever put on antidepressants. I was a young woman, the doctors said, who had learned to take things far too seriously and personally. I was a wreck. But over time, I learned to turn around my tendency to always think negatively and have found happiness. Running has been a big part of what helped me do that. It greatly improved my self-esteem and self-image, gave me an outlet, helped me cope with stress, gave me something I could control and be proud of, gave me endorphins and a high I could always count on. While I know how hard it can be just to get out of bed when you are depressed, if you can, just get your shoes on and get out that door. Just take a few steps; just start to run. You will see what it can do for you. Science has exhaustively concluded that running is as effective as or more effective than antidepressants in the treatment of depression. Study upon study has shown its incredible effects. If I didn't start running, I honestly don't know how I ever would have made it through the depressive episodes of my life.

RUNNING AS A LIFELONG TOOL

It wasn't until I had to stop running for over a month following a tonsillectomy that I realized just how significant its impact had been on my life. I went crazy; I got so depressed. I needed my runs. Many runners claim they are "addicted" to running—I am one of them. While scientists dispute whether this is a purely psychological addiction or a physical one based on the chemicals released during exercise, there is no doubt in my mind that you can become addicted to running. For me, I get weepy, sad, emotional, testy, and unable to deal with stress without regular runs. When my husband and I were dating I had to take a week off due to an injury. After about five days, he said, "When can you start running again?" He was reacting to my testiness. That was when he finally understood what running does for me. I hate to make running sound like a drug with all this talk of addiction. The truth is, running can bring you to a new level of happiness—and once that has happened, it's hard to let it go.

DEBBIE'S STORY: FIGHTING DEPRESSION

Debbie Hansen, 32, McMinnville, Oregon

Before her life was interrupted by a severe bout of depression at age 22, Debbie Hansen was a confident, happy young woman. But when her long-term college boyfriend told her he no longer wanted to marry her, her world began to crumble. Things would get worse before they got better. Here's her story of running helped her to get her life back on course:

The day he told me he no longer wanted to marry me . . . well, to say that I lost it would be an understatement. Now that I am healthy I can't even believe that threw me like it did, but I was a mess. I cried all the time. I could not eat. My sleeping patterns were bizarre. I was not myself. I felt as if I was on the edge of this strange emotional cliff with one foot hanging off. And some moments I thought I was going to be just fine and then a moment later the slightest wrong glance or word would push me over the edge. I saw my doctor, who prescribed two Prozac to get me through the day. It worked, but it was an expensive option and made me feel odd. I did gradually get back on my feet, but I began to notice the Prozac made me a little jittery. So I went off it, with a doctor's prescribed plan. I started dating again and things were going well until that relationship ended. I started back into the tailspin. I had to be put back on Prozac (though a smaller dose). I then took up running.

I had never been athletic. I had always been a little heavy, though not huge. The depression and Prozac had caused me to drop weight quickly, and since I was suddenly slim I took up running to try to maintain my new figure. After about a month of that I no longer needed Prozac. That was five years ago. I have now completed two marathons (one in under four hours). I am not the same person I was then. I truly believe it is no longer possible for me to slip into depression. I haven't been to "the edge" for years. I think the reason is a much-improved sense of confidence and power from within—and running gave me that. I now run between five and six times a week. It is my time for myself to think, to enjoy the sights and smells around me, to organize my day or my life . . . I don't know if there was a chemical or hormonal shift that took place as I increased my mileage, but whatever it was, it is all mine. The loss of a boyfriend or a job or anything else will never hit me like that again.

CHAPTER FOUR

PMS, Menopause, and Running

Hormones. From the time they start raging inside our bodies in puberty, these body chemicals have a huge impact on the emotional health of women. Between premenstrual syndrome (PMS), pregnancy, postpartum depression, and menopause, the majority of our adult lives can be spent coping with hormonal ups and downs. The physical side effects of these fluctuations can be severe—even potentially fatal—and the psychological effects can be, at times, debilitating. According to the American College of Obstetrics and Gynecology (ACOG), 85 percent of menstruating women suffer from PMS, with 5 to 10 percent of those women debilitated by their symptoms. Meanwhile, the North American Menopause Society estimates that 2 million women in Canada and the United States reached menopause in the year 2000. These conditions impact every facet of our lives, from our relationships, to our careers, to the bottom-line quality of our lives. Struggling to cope, women around the world have turned to countless remedies, from crushed flower petals, to antidepressants, to diets. One remedy that is sometimes overlooked, however, is aerobic exercise.

PREMENSTRUAL SYNDROME

Before we get into how running can help women suffering from PMS, it's important to define what we are talking about. PMS is characterized by a number of physical and psychological symptoms associated with our monthly cycles. These symptoms may include depression, irritability, bloating, water retention, abdominal cramps, breast tenderness, nausea, increased appetite, and a number of other physical and psychological conditions. These symptoms can start anytime during the menstrual cycle, but typically appear 7 to 14 days before menstruation. These side effects can have a significant impact on the lives of women, with some reporting that their relationships and careers have been jeopardized. The predominant method used to diagnose PMS is charting. A special chart outlines the various symptoms down one side, with the days of the month numbered along the top. Women are asked to color in the boxes according to how severely each symptom was experienced on each day. The patterns are then assessed to determine if in fact the symptoms are PMS.

What Causes PMS?

The exact cause of PMS is not known. In fact, it is not even known for sure whether hormonal ups and downs are to blame; this is, however, the leading theory among scientists and doctors. But according to the ACOG, researchers do know that the hormones progesterone, testosterone, and estrogen are involved. It is also known that there are changes in levels of serotonin, a brain chemical involved in mood, in women suffering from PMS symptoms.

How Can Running Help?

You feel bloated, tired, cranky, and achy. The last thing you feel like doing is suiting up and going outside for some physical activity. The truth is, however, that this may just be the best thing for you. Running helps relieve cramps, water retention, stress, emotional upheaval, and many of the other symptoms of PMS. In fact, aerobic exercise was listed as a key pillar of treatment in the ACOG's March 2000 PMS treatment guidelines. Eating a complex-carbohydrate diet and nutritional supplements were two other lifestyle changes the ACOG recommended.

Researchers believe the increased blood flow generated by aerobic exercise helps alleviate PMS symptoms by decreasing bloating and fluid buildup. They also believe that beta-endorphins created during exercise can help our mood. And aerobic exercise can relieve muscle tension in our bodies. Running has a positive impact on our self-esteem and body image, while helping us relax and get away from the problems in our lives. Researchers believe that all these benefits of exercise come together to provide some relief from PMS symptoms.

Several studies have shown the effectiveness of using running and aerobic exercise to treat the symptoms of PMS. A study published in the *European Journal of Applied Physiology and Occupational Physiology* in 1986 found that a moderate running training program significantly decreased PMS symptoms during a three-month trial. Meanwhile, researchers at the University of Queensland, Australia, in 1994 found that exercise had a "significant" impact on the negative moods and physical symptoms across the menstrual cycle. The researchers studied 97 exercisers and 159 nonexercisers. The women completed the Menstrual Distress Questionnaire and the Differential Emotions Scale before, during, and after their periods. The regular exercisers also showed better concentration, less behavioral change, and less physical pain associated with PMS. And in a 1995 study of menstrual cycle symptom changes in competitive sportswomen, exercisers, and sedentary women, scientists at the University in Nottingham, U.K., found that exercise may protect women from negative mood changes related to their cycles. The moods and physical symptoms of 143 women were observed for five days in each of the three phases of the menstrual cycle (midcycle, premenstrual, and menstrual). There were 35 competitive sportswomen, 33 high exercisers, 36 low exercisers, and 39 sedentary women. The high exercisers reported the fewest negative menstrual-related symptoms and the sedentary women reported the most. The study concluded that women who frequently exercise might to some extent be protected from deterioration of mood before and during menstruation.

The Melpomene Institute's Judy Mahle Lutter says not enough is known about the cause of PMS to determine exactly why running can help alleviate symptoms. But, she adds, the endorphin release and the sense that you are taking control of the situation both likely play roles. "Beyond the chemical change, there's a feeling that you are able to do something about it. It's important to get out of that situation when your body doesn't feel like it can do anything." Lutter stresses, however, that nothing is a cure-all. So while aerobic exercise may help alleviate PMS symptoms in some women, there is no magic wand in the treatment of the syndrome.

Running May Be Your Escape

During that major depressive episode I wrote about in the last chapter, I was also diagnosed with PMS. My depression seemed to get worse right before my period. The PMS clinic at the hospital I went to gave me a prescription that included a low-caffeine and -sugar diet, not drinking alcohol, and *exercise*! I couldn't believe it. I thought that with all the research done on PMS, they must have come up with some kind of wonder drugs to make me better. What I didn't realize then was that their research had done just that. While there are some drugs that have been proven to be effective in treating PMS symptoms, exercise has proven to be one of the most effective methods of treatment.

Each month, I try to make sure I don't miss any runs in the week before my period. And when I find that I'm getting a little too strung out and emotional, I often realize my period is on its way and I haven't managed to squeeze in any runs the last couple of days. Once I go for a run, I feel much better. My mother, in fact, used to tell me to go for a run whenever I'd get a little difficult to manage in my PMS week. Aside from the emotional benefits, it also makes me feel physically better. However, my cycle can have a negative impact on the quality of my runs. Often I'll run slower and feel more tired. I cut myself some slack, though. I remind myself that it's just important to get a run in, no matter how unsuccessful. I always feel better when I get back.

MENOPAUSE

One of life's cruel ironies is that just as we stop menstruating, leaving PMS behind, we are thrown a potentially even more disruptive hormonal curveball: menopause. Hitting at the average age of 52, menopause is the time when our ovaries stop releasing eggs, causing a significant decline in the production of estrogen and other hormones. The perimenopausal stage starts 2 to 10 years before this time. Side effects of menopause include moodiness, depression, trouble concentrating, trouble remembering things, changes in the menstrual cycle, hot flashes, loss of libido, weight gain, fatigue, and many others. More serious physical changes during menopause also result in the increased chance of developing heart disease and osteoporosis. Women can lose up to 20 percent of their bone mass in the first five to seven years after menopause because of the decline in estrogen in the body. That hormonal decline can also be responsible for increasing the risk of heart disease and heart attacks. Cardiovascular disease is the most common cause of death for women in their menopause years.

The Power of Estrogen

When our estrogen levels decrease after menopause, our bones begin to get worn down because the hormone has a protective effect on our bones. Estrogen helps prevent calcium loss by standing in the way of bone-eroding cells called osteoclasts. This hormone also protects our hearts by helping prevent the hardening of, and the collection of plaque inside, our arteries. With lower levels of estrogen, our arteries can harden over time and put us at a greater risk for heart disease and stroke.

How Can Running Help?

While not of help to every woman, and by no means a magic bullet, running and aerobic exercise can help alleviate many of the psychological and physical symptoms of menopause. Many studies have shown that regular exercise can help combat a number of these symptoms, including hot flashes and night sweats, the thinning and irritation of the vagina and urinary tract, depression, insomnia, osteoporosis, and cardiovascular risk factors. Additionally, postmenopausal women who exercise regularly are about half as likely to develop diabetes as their sedentary counterparts.

Judy Mahle Lutter says the Melpomene Institute's studies have shown that the benefits of running during menopause can go beyond the physical. "For the majority of women running is positive because they are feeling so out of control at this time in their lives," she notes. "Some women said it helped with hot flashes, some said it didn't. But most said it did help them take back control of their bodies." While Lutter herself found that menopause was the one time in her life when running didn't help her, many women have found it does, and she encourages menopausal women to take up running if they haven't already. "This may be just the time to start."

Your Mood

Improved mood was the most frequently reported benefit associated with running in a questionnaire survey conducted by the Melpomene Institute and *Runner's World* magazine, published in the magazine in June 1998. A total of 74.5 percent of those women surveyed reported that running made a positive difference in the way they experienced menopause. Improved mood was reported by 30.7 percent. An overall decrease in menopausal symptoms was reported by 24.8 percent. A decrease in stress was reported by 11 percent. Additionally, women who run tend to be better able to keep their weight in a healthy range, which can also have a positive impact on their emotional state.

Your Heart

Running and other aerobic exercise prevents heart disease by improving circulation, strengthening the heart, lowering total cholesterol, and raising good cholesterol. With lowered levels of estrogen taking a toll on your arteries, aerobic exercise can help offset the damage. Women who run or do aerobic exercise through menopause also feel healthier overall. In a review of perimenopausal and postmenopausal women published in *Clinics in Sportsmedicine* in 2000, it was reported that women who exercise regularly throughout their lives are physiologically 20 to 30 years younger than their sedentary counterparts. It suggested women do aerobic exercise three to seven days a week, for 15 to 60 minutes each time.

Your Bones

The best way to prevent osteoporosis and the loss of bone mass during menopause is to build up your bones with exercise and a good diet before the age of 35. Weight-bearing activities, like running, strengthen the bones because the force causes an increase in bone density. But exercise and good nutrition can only help us during a certain window of opportunity. Peak bone mass is reached between the ages of 25 and 35. After that, bone mass starts to decrease. A report presented by an osteoporosis panel of the National Institutes of Health recommended regular exercise, especially resistance and high-impact activities, as the best way to contribute to the development of high peak bone mass.

CHAPTER FIVE

Getting Motivated

A lack of discipline, energy, and time are the top three reasons women don't exercise. That's according to a study conducted by the Melpomene Institute via a questionnaire in a 1996 issue of *Self* magazine. The key to overcoming these obstacles is finding your motivation, or more importantly, staying motivated. If you are motivated, you can become disciplined, you will find the time to exercise, and the running itself will give you more energy. But first you have to get the ball rolling. Getting people motivated has been the hardest aspect of the running clinics I have taught. Inevitably, after the first night of the class, the numbers of those turning out dwindle week after week. Even some of those who come on a regular basis admit to me that they only run when the group is together; they don't seem to find the time (I say *drive*) to do it on their own. And this is so frustrating for me. Not because I see it as a failure on my part to get these people riled up and ready to make running part of their lives, but because I know what they are missing.

GET LEVERAGE

If you are having a hard time getting motivated, you might find your inspiration by thinking about what you will get out of running if you stick to your schedule. Burning about 100 calories every 10 minutes, running can help you shed extra pounds and eat what you want the way few other exercises can. Think about what your body will look like if you stick with the program. Imagine the clothing you could wear, how it will feel on your body, and how you will feel about yourself. As a more immediate reward, think about how you are going to feel when you get back from your run, or even about how good about yourself you'll feel out there pounding the pavement and working toward a goal. You'll come back with a clearer head and a better outlook, feeling revved for the rest of your day. Think about all of the benefits of running for your emotional health. Think about the calmer, happier person you'll be if you stick with your plan. You might want to write a list of all the great things that will happen if you make the decision to be motivated and disciplined. Then write a list outlining all the things you envision happening if you *don't* make that change. Perhaps your weight will continue to go up, or you might never run the marathon that has always been a dream of yours. Whatever it is, write it down and think about it. This is all about getting leverage—enough weight behind what you want that you have no choice but to make it happen.

A woman in one of my beginner running clinics used to call herself an "athlete" jokingly. She had bought all of the fancy running clothing and strutted around talking about how she had to get it, since "I'm an athlete now." It was really quite funny—and yet she was following a training plan, running three times a week, working up to a competitive street race. In my mind, she *was* an athlete. I would try to tell her that, but she'd just laugh it off. Meanwhile, I think down deep she fancied the idea of becoming an athlete. She had a picture of what kind of person she'd be if she stuck with the program, and she held that up as her leverage for making sure she kept with it. Needless to say, she was all smiles as she effortlessly ran across the finish line of her first 5K race. Perhaps drawing a similar picture in your mind will help you stick with it. The key is to find the leverage you need to make it happen.

MAKE A PROMISE TO YOURSELF

There will always be a reason not to run. In this world, there's always something else you could be doing. What you need to do is make it a priority. Make a commitment to yourself, to your body, to your mind. An hour and a half a week is all you need to make a significant difference in your life. Anyone can find that kind of time in her week. Plan ahead; schedule your runs when you know you have time, when you are not tired, when there is someone to take care of the kids. It's a great gift to give to your significant other, children, friends, and coworkers. When you are happy and relaxed, all of those around you benefit. You will be a better worker, mother, sister, friend, spouse, whatever. You will be a better you.

One great way to make running a priority is to make a serious promise to yourself. Make a decision about what your goal should be, figure out what you will have to do to make that happen, then promise yourself you will do it. It's a good idea to write this promise down someplace special. You don't want it to be swept under the carpet with other good intentions of days gone by. You want this one to stick. So write it down in your journal or write it on a piece of paper and stick it someplace you'll see it often. Do what you have to do to give this promise some significance. You might even want to tell your family or friends about it and ask them to help you stick to your plan. Whenever you find yourself thinking you don't want to go for a run, think about what that promise means to you. Think about your goal and remind yourself that you will not get there if you don't follow the plan you have set out for yourself. Remember that you owe it to yourself to stick with your plan. Undoubtedly you will not always be successful at doing this. If you fall off the wagon, get right back on. Don't think that just because one week, or even two, is blown, it's not worth continuing on. Just get back to it and focus on moving forward.

SET OUT A SCHEDULE

In order to stay motivated, you have to know exactly how you are going to accomplish your goals. You need a plan. Using the schedules outlined in this book, you can set out a 10- to 16-week schedule to get you started. Work out how many runs each week you need to do, how far each run should be, what intensity you want from those runs, and what days will be rest days. It's a good idea to make up a chart outlining the upcoming weeks so that you can check off the runs as you do them, keep track of your mileage, and jot down how each run felt. It can be very inspiring to have a physical display of how far you've come. Setting out a rigid plan can also make it easier to stick with it by giving you less room for cheating. If you don't know exactly when and how far you need to run, it's easier to just not go. Give it the weight you'd give a doctor's appointment or a business meeting. You wouldn't miss those, would you? No, you wouldn't want to let down the people who are expecting you to be there. So why let yourself down? Set out a schedule and stick to it.

MAKING THE TIME

Most women today feel hard-pressed to squeeze anything more into their schedules, let alone three 30-minute workouts each week. But it can be done. Right now there are working moms with three kids training for the Iron Man Triathlon in Hawaii. How do they find the time? Simple: They make the time. It might mean getting up an hour before anyone else does, or seeking out three different people to watch the kids for half an hour, but you can find the time if you really want to. Some women feel guilty about taking time out for themselves, but what they fail to realize is just how much better a mom, wife, employee, they will be if they invest in their emotional and physical health this way.

For women on the go, planning exactly when you are going to run is critical. You know your weekly schedule; don't paint yourself into a corner by not planning for your runs ahead of time. You might have to work it into something else you are doing. Baby Jogger strollers make it easy to take smaller children out on the run with you. You can run to the doctor's office, run to the grocery store, or run during your lunch break. There are lots of ways to work those workouts into your day without throwing your schedule into complete chaos.

Tips to Work Running into Your Schedule

- ✔ Run to work and take the bus home.
- ✔ Take running shoes on trips.
- ✔ Run with kids.
- ✔ Create a baby-sitting group with local moms.

JUST DO IT, DON'T MAKE EXCUSES

Many things can come up that might make you put off your run to another day. This can happen day after day unless you have made your running a priority and have made the decision to stop making excuses. "I'm too tired, the house is a mess, I have so much work to do"—there's always a reason not to go for your runs. What you need to do is think of all the reasons to go for your run. When you hear yourself making an excuse, just stop. Put on your shoes and go for a run. Despite being the hugely successful slogan for a shoe company, *Just do it* has always been a powerful mantra for me. Whenever I'm sitting there thinking about whether or not to do something I know I ought to, I tell myself to just do it. "Don't think about it," I say to myself, "just do it." Just do it. Go. Now. Don't think. Go. Now. Ultimately, there is no other way. You need to find a way to make yourself get out that door. Remember: No excuses.

REWARD YOURSELF

Improved emotional and physical health are more than enough reward for making running a part of your life. But sometimes it can make the journey a little more fun to add to it a few more rewards for yourself. For instance, after every marathon, I allow myself to eat anything I want. Primarily this includes a big bag of barbecue-flavored Fritos. These evil, but tasty, little things were a big part of what helped me pack on the pounds in my teens, so I don't allow myself to eat them normally. But if I told myself I could never eat them again, it would be too much to take. If I successfully train for and run a marathon, though, I get to have a bag. I also treat myself to a nice breakfast after my long Sunday runs during marathon training. You might want to give yourself a different kind of reward—for instance, taking a few days off from running if you don't miss a scheduled run for a certain number of weeks. Pick something that is of value to you, something that would be worth working for, then give it to yourself. Hard work deserves a reward.

MAKE IT FUN

I like to play a little game with myself to make sure I do all of my runs each week. In the beginning I told myself that no matter what, I had to get in three runs each week. So if I chose to be lazy on Monday, that was fine. Tuesday too. Wednesday and Thursday could go by, but come Friday I would have no choice but to run. Ditto for Saturday and Sunday. (While I would suggest spreading your runs out across the week, this is what I had to do just to get my butt out the door.) I did most of my "bad" eating on the weekend anyway, so this worked well for me. You may have to play similar games with yourself to make sure you put in your runs. Maybe you need a run club or partner; maybe you need a heart rate monitor that will beep at you endlessly if more than two days have gone by without a run!

There are also lots of great ways to make running fun. You can pick fun routes or vary the speeds of your workout to spice things up. During the Toronto film festival, I run through the part of town where all the celebrities stay in the hope of seeing someone famous. (Unfortunately, I mostly come across other people who are doing the same.) You might also want to consider running like a kid, arms and legs flailing all over the place. Listening to a mixed tape of your favorite inspiring songs is another way to find motivation. Figure out whatever it is you need to have fun running. It will help keep you motivated and on course toward your goals.

GETTING OUT THE DOOR

I know how hard it is to get those shoes on. Even after three marathons, I still sometimes whine and complain until I actually get out that door. And then, sometimes, I continue to whine until the first 10 minutes have passed, and I get into a groove. But I have to tell you, once I'm in that groove I am so glad I did it. It makes the whole day a better day. I feel proud of myself, less guilty about what I eat, and more in control of my life. And when you stick with it over time, your body changes, your mind changes, all for the better. But saying all that won't get someone out there pounding the pavement. The truth is, I don't know what will. What I *can* say is that if you make running a part of your life, you'll never be the same again. So make yourself a promise. Set yourself a goal of a race a few months down the road. Put in your three runs a week and slowly work toward that goal. I guarantee that once you cross that finish line, we'll have hooked you for life. You'll be a runner and you won't ever want to stop.

MARLO'S STORY: TAKING BACK CONTROL

Marlo Palko, 30, Toronto

Diagnosed with a rare form of ovarian cancer, Marlo Palko's life was shaken to its foundation at age 24. Although it was a highly treatable cancer with an impressive cure rate, beating it meant three months of aggressive chemotherapy. In one fell swoop, she says, she went from taking a healthy body—and mind—for granted to being a cancer patient. After surviving her bout with cancer, Marlo decided to train for a half-marathon. Running, she found, helped her feel reconnected with the body that she once felt betrayed her and helped her regain her emotional strength. Here's her story:

As my hair fell out and I acquired the dark-eyed, swollen-faced look of my cancer, I also had to put my faith, and my life, in the hands of a team of strangers. I suddenly became a very passive player in my own life. I did what I could. I read about meditation, visualization, detoxification, and all the possible ways I might participate in my own healing—but in truth, I was beholden to the magic of medicine. In my quest to get better, I merely got sicker and sicker. Always one to be strong and active, the cancer-patient me was grateful for wheelchairs and bed-

rest. At my worst, I could face no more than one flight of stairs and had to be helped on the short walk around my own block. It is a devastating moment when you realize that there really is no invincibility of youth—and that the only path to health is going to take you right through that valley of God-awful frailty. Because I had not been sick prior to my diagnosis, the side effects were even more difficult to manage—I railed against a body I seemed to have lost control of and no longer even recognized.

But treatment came to a victorious end when, on February 14, 1996, I saw my first drug-free day. Immediately, I went back to my life. I returned to work; I went on trips; I tried to pick up where I had left off. But every year, on Valentine's Day, my family and I have faithfully celebrated the passing of another cancer-free year. And each year, I celebrate just that much stronger than I was the year before.

This year, I celebrated my five-year anniversary—the milestone at which my doctors declared me cured and I was able to cut my ties with checkups and life as a patient. As I approached this mark, I also began to run. The coincidence of my five-year anniversary and running is just that—coincidence. I had agreed to take on the 21K challenge partly as a dare and partly as a result of one too many drinks one night with friends. Until then, I had been a sporadic runner at best and was more trying to save face than really take on this gargantuan feat. So in January 2001 I started training. It was cold, and I was often as miserable as the weather, but each run, quite unexpectedly, reignited something in me that I had forgotten I had—a passion and determination to take back control of my own body and my own destiny. When I ran, it was the moment in my day when I reconnected to a body that I thought had failed me. With every increased distance, I trusted a little more in the body I had regarded as a traitor. And the glory of it was, that 3K was as triumphant as 20K. In the aches and pains of long-distance running, I recaptured a sense of myself that I had surrendered five years before. When I ran, I knew it was all about me—one more step was possible because I said it was so. I had to answer to no greater power than my own will. And as I ran farther and farther, I marveled at my own strength—and the sheer victory of being able to power that run on my own steam. As I grew stronger as a runner, I spent more and more time with my body: listening to its signals, rewarding it for a job well done, testing its limits. In that process, I reintroduced myself to me and realized that my body wasn't a failure—it had just changed.

I have always maintained that my life after cancer compels me to be better and braver and stronger than I was before—or else my surviving was in vain. And my running has given me back the sense of fearlessness and audacity and accomplishment that I had put away. My running has made me bolder and given me a confidence I didn't even know I possessed. It has taught me that there is much to the art of celebration and that sometimes a heaving chest and sore legs are there merely to force you to remember that you are alive—and to remember the days they couldn't celebrate with you.

So when I crossed the finish line of the Ottawa half-marathon in May 2001, I crossed triumphant and strong. I ran that day not to leave my struggle behind, but to celebrate the victory of it, to reconcile illness with strength, to dare myself to do it, and to know that my mind and body were one again, and that together they could overcome. As is the saying, "You are a survivor because of the way you live, not because you didn't die."

PART II

ON THE ROAD

Taking Control of Your Mind with Your Body

CHAPTER SIX

Hitting the Road

When we were children, many of us ran everywhere we went. Dashing here and there was second nature to us; we had seemingly endless stores of energy. But as adults, running is rarely that easy. With our busy lives and older bodies, it takes planning, structure, and know-how to fit a productive run into the day. And since our goal is no longer just to get to the playground before everyone else, we need to set out a game plan in order to meet our objectives in running. This chapter will take a look at the basics of hitting the road: how fast to run, good running form, where to run, the different kinds of running, and how much to run and when. Whether your goal is to work up to running a few minutes at a time or to run your next race faster, it's important to make sure you've got the basics of hitting the pavement covered.

TAKE IT SLOW

Once you've experienced the emotional and physical benefits of running, it's easy to want to do as much as possible as soon as you can. However, it's critical at all stages of your running career to progress slowly. The biggest mistake all runners, and beginner runners in particular, make is to do too much, too fast, too soon. That's the easiest way to get hurt and be forced to cut down on your running. That's bound to be a serious disappointment to anyone who has grown dependent on her runs. Once you've built up the motivation to tackle a training program of any kind, it can be depressing to have to stop, not to mention quite difficult to build up the drive to do it all again down the road. Also, upping your mileage too quickly can lead to burnout or cause you to get discouraged if suddenly you reach a point in the training program that does seem too difficult. So be smart. Take it slow. Even if you are tempted to kick it up a notch, don't. Follow your schedule as planned and work up slowly. The general rule is to increase your mileage by no more than 10 or 15 percent per week. That's the best way to ensure you don't get hurt and to make sure you don't put too much pressure on yourself. Following this rule of thumb will help ensure you enjoy your running and you get the most out of its emotional and health benefits.

Pace

Holding back on your pace is another critical element of any running program. Beginner runners often run too fast, then wonder why it's such an unpleasant experience. Your muscles, heart, and lungs may be able to let you run at a fast speed, but that doesn't mean it will be comfortable. With any program, you want 90 percent of your running to be done at conversation pace, meaning that you should be able to carry on a conversation for most of your run. For the first 10 minutes or so of a run it can sometimes be hard to do that, but after that point, if you can't carry on a conversation, it's time to slow down. While running faster will ultimately translate into better race times and burning more calories down the road, picking up the pace needs to be done strategically and, again, slowly. You need to build a base of at least a year of strong, comfortable mileage before working on your speed. Also, for reasons I'll outline further later in this chapter, the most amount of fat is burned at conversation pace.

Striking a Balance

While it is very important to take it slow, I must say you can sometimes take it too slow. Make sure that you are following a training schedule that progresses slowly, but still at a pace that is somewhat challenging. It is possible to underestimate your ability when initially deciding on a training plan. So if you really feel as though you should be doing more, move up to the next training schedule or make your own alterations to the schedule to tailor the program to your needs. But if at any time you find what you are doing too challenging, back off and reassess the situation. Listen to your body and stop if anything hurts. You will have to differentiate between what is normal pain for starting a running program and what is something more serious. Stitches are quite common and par for the course when you are getting into shape and putting a lot of stress on a system that is not used to it. Muscle pain is also quite common. If it's in the meaty parts of your body, it's probably just the natural stiffness and soreness that comes with working your muscles. Your muscles actually suffer microscopic tears during a workout, which are later healed when you eat protein. This is how your muscles get larger. So it's natural and expected to feel pain in these areas. You should be concerned, however, if the pain you feel is around a joint, tendon, or very bony area like your knees, ankles, and hips. (See chapter 12 for more information about running injuries.)

CHARTING YOUR COURSE

Before starting any fitness regimen, it is critical to consult with your doctor. Even if you don't feel you are overweight, your heart, lungs, and muscles may not be ready to function at the level you think they can. Take the following programs in to your physician and discuss where she thinks you should be able to start. This is especially important for anyone with any serious health problems or a history of health problems.

The charts below outline five programs for a range of beginner runners, from those who have yet to run one step to those who can run several minutes without stopping. Feel free to move your workout days around, using these charts as a guide only. If you can already run for several minutes at a time, you may want to follow the advanced 5K plan, or perhaps consider the 10K program. I've provided schedules for both the half- and full marathons for those who are ready to tackle these larger races, but also for those in the beginning of their running careers. These goals really are attainable.

The schedules can be adapted to suit your own sense of where you are at in your running career. Don't feel you have to follow them exactly. If you'd like to move up to the next schedule, or down, do it. You can also adjust the schedules slightly to reflect your individual abilities. In any case, do commit to a program that increases in difficulty each week. As is reflected in the beginner schedules, time is more important than mileage. Still, it can be nice to know how far you are going. You can chart how far your runs are by riding the distance in your car, with a pedometer on your bike, or—my favorite method—using a MapArt CD-ROM to chart the distance exactly.

HOW TO MOVE

When we ran as kids, we just went; we didn't think about form, stride, and the like. But as adults, it's important that we work on having good form to avoid injuries and make our runs more pleasant.

Form

The key to good form is symmetry. You don't want any part of your body flailing out or leaning to one side. You want your head upright, your shoulders back, your hips forward, your legs flowing forward, your stomach tucked in. You also want to land on your heel, then roll forward and push off with your toes, preferably with your feet landing about hip-width apart. Kicking one leg out, leaning to one side, and other lopsided tendencies should be avoided. Still, it is true that some of the best runners in the world have atrocious form. Many a sportscaster has marveled at how they can move so fast. It could be argued, however, that these people are already naturally gifted runners with bodies that were built for running. If the average Joe runner tried to run with some of these quirks, he'd probably develop some sort of related injury.

Stride

The length of your stride is something that should initially figure itself out. Don't worry too much about it. Just go with the flow. When you do start to think about picking up your pace, however, you don't want to change the length of your stride. Stretching your legs out in front of you farther than is natural is a fast way to hurt yourself. Also, biomechanically you actually slow yourself down this way because your heel actually acts as a brake when you land. So when you want to go faster, it's your stride rate that you want to increase. That means you want to increase the number of times your legs turn over. Research has shown that beginner runners tend to hit the ground with their feet 150 to 160 times per minute, while 180 times is ideal. Counting the number of times your feet hit the ground, however, sounds to me like one of the fastest ways to make a run unpleasant. While you might want to count once in a while to keep tabs on where you are, I'd suggest just making an effort to turn your legs over more often.

HOW TO BREATHE

How you breathe when you run is one of the most critical elements of having a pleasant run. Not only can effective breathing help prevent stitches and alleviate those that come, but it is vital to being able to relax into your run. (I go into this in greater detail in chapter 7.) I like to tell people to breathe in a pattern that they've worked out ahead of time. You'll actually figure out what pattern is best for you just by trying it out on the run. I like to breathe "in-in, out, in-in, out." While it's not possible to breathe in totally through your nose, it works best for many people to breathe in mostly through the nose, then out the mouth. This is particularly important in the wintertime when cooler temperatures can be hard on your throat. The goal here is to get to a point where your breathing is effortless and you can simply relax into your run.

WHERE TO RUN

The surfaces you run on can make a big difference to how your body and mind survive the weekly mileage you've chosen. The following is an outline of the pros and cons of all the running surfaces you'll have to choose from.

Sidewalks

Concrete is estimated to be 10 percent harder than asphalt, and far harder than natural surfaces, so sidewalks are not the recommended surface to run on. However, runners, particularly women runners, sometimes have no choice. In order to stay safe from cars and from those up to no good, women often have to stick to populated areas, which often means the sidewalk. If you can find a safe alternative, however, use it.

Roads

While not as hard as concrete, asphalt is still not an ideal choice for runners. Roads are also cambered, or curved on the edges to allow for rain runoff. If you run on the same side of the road all the time, with one side of your body contracted because it's on the higher end of the road, and the other side extended because it's lower, you can get injuries as a result. So if you are going to run on one side of the road, make sure you run on the other too. Also, don't forget about the cars. Drivers too often see the road as their turf alone. Make sure drivers see you, and keep your wits about you if you choose to run on the road.

Trails

Trails are by far one of the best places to run. With wood chips or earth under your feet, you have a great cushioned yet firm surface. Along with those natural bonuses, however, you also get tree roots, rocks, and other bits of nature that make the surface unstable and ripe for a sprained ankle or a spill. With a trail you'll also face the issue of personal safety. Trails tend to be isolated, putting you at potential risk for an attack. If you do head for the trails, think about bringing a run buddy along.

Track

Like roads, tracks have a cambered surface that sets you up for injury if you don't run as often in one direction as you do the other. Most tracks put up an arrow, which changes the direction of the track every day. You will have to make sure you aren't heading to the track every other day, however, to avoid related overuse injuries. Outdoor tracks tend to have less of a cambered surface. Indoor tracks can also be smelly and warm, but can make it very easy to chart your distance. They can also be safer, in some cases, than running outside.

Beaches

Running on the beach can be quite pleasant and fun, but you can be setting yourself up for Achilles tendonitis. The loose surface of the sand allows your Achilles tendon to stretch out farther than it would on a harder surface, which can lead to problems.

Hills

Hills are something beginner runners like to avoid. While this is often because of the level of difficulty involved, it's also a good idea because you can hurt yourself if you don't have a strong running base running under your belt. Once you do, however, throwing a few hills into your route can spice things up and make you stronger. Don't forget to let yourself have a few downhills too.

WHAT ZONE ARE YOU IN?

As I have already stressed, you want the majority of your running to be at conversation pace. To understand why, let's take a short lesson in body chemistry. The first thing you need to know is that when we run, we use two kinds of metabolism (chemical methods of making energy) to fuel our bodies.

Aerobic Metabolism

Aerobic metabolism is the method our bodies use to fuel low-intensity activities, including running at a conversation pace. Using glucose or blood sugar (stored as glycogen in your muscles and liver) and oxygen, this kind of metabolism can go on providing our bodies with fuel for hours on end. However, this method can only give us fuel quite slowly. Aerobic metabolism also has very few by-products like lactic acid, which makes our muscles ache after it accumulates. Only small amounts of lactic acid are formed during aerobic metabolism, which means we can clear it away before it starts to hurt us. When you are in the aerobic zone you also burn the most fat. An example of aerobic exercise is running at a pace of 10 minutes per mile.

A good way to know if you are in this aerobic zone is to calculate your maximum heart rate. For women, subtract your age from 226, and you will get your maximum heart rate (the approximate maximum number of times your heart should beat in a minute). The aerobic zone is from about 60 percent of your maximum heart rate to 85 percent. You can then take your heart rate on the run, or use a heart rate monitor. To take your heart rate on your own, wait until you have been running for 10 minutes or more, then stop and quickly press your pointer finger and middle finger against the side of your throat. Count the number of times your heart beats in 15 seconds, then multiply this by four to get your total for a minute. Compare that number to 65 to 85 percent of your maximum heart rate to make sure you are "in the zone." Heart rate monitors can make this process easier. These devices are bands that wrap around your chest to monitor your heart. They send a message to an accompanying wristwatch, which will actually beep if you are not inside the aerobic zone. (For more information on heart rate monitors, see chapter 9.)

A much simpler way of checking if you are in the aerobic zone is to simply make sure you can talk when you are running. Staying in this aerobic zone is not essential; it is merely the best zone to be in for maximum fat burning and the most enjoyable runs. Running slower than this won't give your body a real workout and running faster, as we will see in the next section, is best reserved for special training geared for improved race times.

Anaerobic Metabolism

When your running starts to demand greater amounts of energy from you at a faster rate—for instance, when you run fast or have been running for several hours—you switch over to something called anaerobic metabolism. This happens when your body can't process oxygen fast enough to fuel your activity. This method of creating energy in your body can produce a lot of energy very quickly, but it has a few major drawbacks. The first is that this kind of metabolism creates a lot of byproducts like lactic acid, which accumulates in your muscles and makes you very sore. Also, this kind of metabolism can only go on for two minutes at a time. Yes, that's right, two minutes! If anaerobic exercise continues beyond this point, so much lactic acid will form that it will affect your ability to create energy and you will be forced to stop. An example of this is one shift in a hockey game or a 400-meter sprint.

Anaerobic Threshold

When you are running, you are never totally using aerobic metabolism or anaerobic metabolism; you are using a combination of both at all times. There is a point, however, at which you switch from predominantly using aerobic metabolism to using mostly anaerobic. This is called your anaerobic threshold. Runners looking to beat their best race times or run a marathon work on pushing back this threshold so they can stay in the aerobic zone longer. By training at high intensities, you teach your body to maintain this level of effort despite the lactic acid. Your body has a maximum rate at which you can use oxygen (called your VO2 max) and by training this way, you extend this rate. Ultimately, your body also learns to be more efficient at producing energy and at clearing away the buildup of lactic acid. You do all this with something called speedwork.

The Right Zone

Armed with the scientific background, you can now see why I encourage you to do most of your running at a lower intensity. You don't want to go anaerobic, because then you will have to stop. And when you do want to practice going anaerobic, it should be done in the form of properly planned speedwork. If nothing else, you should run at conversation pace because it's comfortable and the best way to burn fat. So the next time you think you are not running fast enough, think again. You now know better.

TYPES OF RUNNING

While beginner runners should stick to whatever pace and distance is comfortable for them, there are a number of other kinds of running that you can incorporate into your training as you progress. These alternative styles of running are a good way to spice things up when your regular runs get boring or to help build strength and speed when you get into racing.

- ✔ **STEADY RUNS:** This kind of running will make up the bulk of your runs. It involves nice, steady runs of relatively short distance, which will ultimately develop your stamina.

- ✔ **LONG RUNS:** Long runs are typically about 15K or longer. They are usually done as a part of a half-marathon or full-marathon training plan. They help increase your capillary network and raise your anaerobic threshold.

- ✔ **FARTLEK:** *Fartlek* means "speedplay" in Swedish. It refers to a kind of running where you insert bursts of increased speed into the overall flow of a run. You are running the entire time, but you go faster every now and then. Some people do it between two light poles, two trees, or two streetlights. It's up to you. This kind of running will improve your speed and strength.

- ✔ **TEMPO RUNS:** Tempo runs involve running relatively short distances at an increased pace. An example would be running three sets of 2,000 meters at a faster pace than you are used to. Again, this will work on your speed and strength, and push back that anaerobic threshold.

- ✔ **HILL REPEATS:** Hill repeats are usually done when you are preparing for a longer race or want to shave extra minutes off a shorter race. They involve running up a long hill several times in a row. You should start with 4 repeats and work up to as many as 12. These repeats build your muscles and can ultimately make you a faster runner. You should run about 3 or 4 kilometers before and after a hill repeat session.

- ✔ **SPEED INTERVALS:** Speed intervals are fast runs over a short distance. For example, you would run 5 to 12 repeats of about a mile at 85 percent of your maximum heart rate or higher. This kind of running improves your speed and raises your anaerobic threshold.

You should have at least one year's worth of mileage under your belt before you consider partaking in any speedwork. It can be a fast way to hurt yourself, so if you aren't feeling in peak shape, it's something you should stay away from. However, these speedwork options can be quite fun and helpful in working on your pace.

TRAINING PROGRAMS FOR A 5K RACE

Everyone begins a running program at a different level of physical fitness. The training program here, for a 5K race, begins with an all-walking regimen if you feel you're not ready to run just yet. If you think you can manage running for a minute at a time, or three minutes, I have included training programs for these levels. Select the schedule you feel looks right for you.

W= Walking R= Running X= Repeat # of times

Schedule One: STARTING WITH WALKING

WEEK	MON.	TUES.	WED.	THURS.	FRI.	SAT.	SUN.
1	W 20 min.	Off	W 20 min.	Off	W 20 min.	Off	Off
2	W 20 min.	Off	W 20 min.	Off	W 20 min.	Off	Off
3	W 25 min.	Off	W 25 min.	Off	W 25 min.	Off	Off
4	W 30 min.	Off	W 30 min.	Off	W 30 min.	Off	Off
5	W 15 min., R 1 min., W 15 min.	Off	W 15 min., R 1 min., W 15 min.	Off	W 15 min., R 1 min., W 15 min.	Off	Off

6	W 13 min., R 2 min., W 13 min.	Off	W 13 min., R 2 min., W 13 min.	Off	W 13 min., R 2 min., W 13 min.	Off	Off
7	W 11 min., R 3 min., W 11 min.	Off	W 11 min., R 3 min., W 11 min.	Off	W 11 min., R 3 min., W 11 min.	Off	Off
8	W 8 min., R 3 min. X 3	Off	W 8 min., R 3 min. X 3	Off	W 8 min., R 3 min. X 3	Off	Off
9	W 6 min., R 3 min. X 4	Off	W 6 min., R 3 min. X 4	Off	W 6 min., R 3 min. X 4	Off	Off
10	W 5 min., R 4 min. X 4	Off	W 5 min., R 4 min. X 4	Off	W 5 min., R 4 min. X 4	Off	Off

Schedule Two
STARTING WITH ONE MINUTE OF RUNNING

WEEK	MON.	TUES.	WED.	THURS.	FRI.	SAT.	SUN.
1	W 5 min., (R 1 min. X 4)	Off	W 5 min., (R 1 min. X 4)	Off	W 5 min., (R 1 min. X 4)	Off	Off
2	W 4 min., R 2 min. X 4	Off	W 4 min., R 2 min. X 4	Off	W 4 min., R 2 min. X 4	Off	Off

3	W 3 min., R 3 min. X 4	Off	W 3 min., R 3 min. X 4	Off	W 3 min., R 3 min. X 4	Off	Off
4	W 2 min., R 4 min. X 4	Off	W 2 min., R 4 min. X 4	Off	W 2 min., R 4 min. X 4	Off	Off
5	W 1 min., R 5 min. X 4	Off	W 1 min., R 5 min. X 4	Off	W 1 min., R 5 min. X 4	Off	Off
6	W 1 min., R 6 min. X 4	Off	W 1 min., R 6 min. X 4	Off	W 1 min., R 6 min. X 4	Off	Off
7	W 1 min., R 7 min. X 4	Off	W 1 min., R 7 min. X 4	Off	W 1 min., R 7 min. X 4	Off	Off
8	W 1 min., R 8 min. X 4	Off	W 1 min., R 8 min. X 4	Off	W 1 min., R 8 min. X 4	Off	Off
9	W 1 min., R 9 min. X 3	Off	W 1 min., R 9 min. X 3	Off	W 1 min., R 9 min. X 3	Off	Off
10	W 1 min., R 10 min. X 3	Off	W 1 min., R 10 min. X 3	Off	W 1 min., R 10 min. X 3	Off	Off

Schedule Three: STARTING WITH THREE MINUTES OF RUNNING

WEEK	MON.	TUES.	WED.	THURS.	FRI.	SAT.	SUN.
1	Off	R 3 min., W 1 min. X 5	Off	R 3 min., W 1 min. X 5	Off	R 3 min., W 1 min. X 5	Off
2	Off	R 4 min., W 1 min. X 4	Off	R 4 min., W 1 min. X 4	Off	R 4 min., W 1 min. X 4	Off
3	Off	R 5 min., W 1 min. X 4	Off	R 5 min., W 1 min. X 4	Off	R 5 min., W 1 min. X 4	Off
4	Off	R 6 min., W 1 min. X 4	Off	R 6 min., W 1 min. X 4	Off	R 6 min., W 1 min. X 4	Off
5	Off	R 8 min., W 1 min. X 3	Off	R 8 min., W 1 min. X 3	Off	R 8 min., W 1 min. X 3	Off
6	Off	R 9 min., W 1 min. X 3	Off	R 9 min., W 1 min. X 3	Off	R 9 min., W 1 min. X 3	Off
7	Off	R 10 min., W 1 min. X 3	Off	R 10 min., W 1 min. X 3	Off	R 10 min., W 1 min. X 3	Off

8	Off	R 13 min., W 1 min. X 2	Off	R 13 min., W 1 min. X 2	Off	R 13 min., W 1 min. X 2	Off
9	Off	R 15 min., W 1 min. X 2	Off	R 15 min., W 1 min. X 2	Off	R 15 min., W 1 min. X 2	Off
10	Off	R 25 min.	Off	R 25 min.	Off	R 25 min.	Off

Schedule Four:
STARTING WITH SEVEN MINUTES OF RUNNING

WEEK	MON.	TUES.	WED.	THURS.	FRI.	SAT.	SUN.
1	R 7 min., W 1 min. X 3	Off	R 7 min., W 1 min. X 3	Off	R 7 min., W 1 min. X 3	Off	Off
2	R 8 min., W 1 min. X 3	Off	R 8 min., W 1 min. X 3	Off	R 8 min., W 1 min. X 3	Off	Off
3	R 9 min., W 1 min. X 3	Off	R 9 min., W 1 min. X 3	Off	R 9 min., W 1 min. X 3	Off	Off
4	R 10 min., W 1 min. X 3	Off	R 10 min., W 1 min. X 3	Off	R 10 min., W 1 min. X 3	Off	Off
5	R 15 min., W 1 min. X 2	Off	R 15 min., W 1 min. X 2	Off	R 15 min., W 1 min. X 2	Off	Off

6	R 20 min.	Off	R 20 min.	Off	R 20 min.	Off	Off
7	R 20 min.	Off	R 20 min.	Off	R 20 min.	Off	Off
8	R 25 min.	Off	R 25 min.	Off	R 25 min.	Off	Off
9	R 30 min.	Off	R 30 min.	Off	R 30 min.	Off	Off
10	R 35 min.	Off	R 35 min.	Off	R 35 min.	Off	Off

Schedule Five: STARTING WITH 15 MINUTES OF RUNNING

WEEK	MON.	TUES.	WED.	THURS.	FRI.	SAT.	SUN.
1	R 15 min., W 1 min. X 2	Off	R 15 min., W 1 min. X 2	Off	R 15 min., W 1 min. X 2	Off	Off
2	R 17 min., W 1 min. X 2	Off	R 17 min., W 1 min. X 2	Off	R 17 min., W 1 min. X 2	Off	Off
3	R 20 min., W 1 min., R 15 min.	Off	R 20 min., W 1 min., R 15 min.	Off	R 20 min., W 1 min., R 15 min.	Off	Off
4	R 25 min., W 1 min., R 10 min.	Off	R 25 min., W 1 min., R 10 min.	Off	R 25 min., W 1 min., R 10 min.	Off	Off
5	R 30 min.	Off	R 30 min.	Off	R 30 min.	Off	Off

6	R 33 min.	Off	R 33 min.	Off	R 33 min.	Off	Off
7	R 35 min.	Off	R 35 min.	Off	R 35 min.	Off	Off
8	R 37 min.	Off	R 37 min.	Off	R 37 min.	Off	Off
9	R 40 min.	Off	R 40 min.	Off	R 40 min.	Off	Off
10	R 45 min.	Off	R 45 min.	Off	R 45 min.	Off	Off

TRAINING PROGRAMS FOR A 10K RACE

WEEK	MON.	TUES.	WED.	THURS.	FRI.	SAT.	SUN.
1	Run 3K	Off	Run 3K	Off	Run 4K	Off	Off
2	Run 4K	Off	Run 3K	Off	Run 4K	Off	Off
3	Run 5K	Off	Run 4K	Off	Run 5K	Off	Off
4	Run 6K	Off	Run 5K	Off	Run 6K	Off	Off
5	Run 5K	Off	Run 5K	Off	Run 5K	Off	Run 3K
6	Run 6K	Off	Run 5K	Off	Run 6K	Off	Run 3K
7	Run 7K	Off	Run 7K	Off	Run 5K	Off	Run 4K
8	Run 8K	Off	Run 5K	Off	Run 8K	Off	Run 5K
9	Run 9K	Off	Run 8K	Off	Run 9K	Off	Run 3K
10	Run 10K	Off	Run 9K	Off	Run 8K	Off	Race Day

10K SCHEDULE (MILES)

WEEK	MON.	TUES.	WED.	THURS.	FRI.	SAT.	SUN.
1	2 miles	Off	2 miles	Off	2.5 miles	Off	Off
2	2.5 miles	Off	2 miles	Off	2.5 miles	Off	Off
3	3 miles	Off	2.5 miles	Off	3 miles	Off	Off
4	3 miles	Off	3 miles	Off	3.5 miles	Off	Off
5	3 miles	Off	3 miles	Off	3 miles	Off	2 miles
6	3.5 miles	Off	3 miles	Off	3.5 miles	Off	2 miles
7	4 miles	Off	4 miles	Off	3 miles	Off	2.5 miles
8	5 miles	Off	3 miles	Off	5 miles	Off	3 miles
9	5.5 miles	Off	5 miles	Off	5 miles	Off	2 miles
10	6 miles	Off	5.5 miles	Off	5 miles	Off	Race 13 miles

SAMPLE TRAINING PROGRAM FOR HALF-MARATHON (KILOMETERS)

WEEK	MON.	TUES.	WED.	THURS.	FRI.	SAT.	SUN.
1	Off	3K	5K	3K	6K	Off	6K
2	Off	3K	6K	3K	6K	Off	6K
3	Off	3K	6K	3K	6K	Off	8K
4	Off	4K	6K	4K	6K	Off	8K
5	Off	4K	6K	5K	6K	Off	10K

6	Off	3K	7K	5K	6K	Off	10K
7	Off	3K	7K	5K	6K	Off	10K
8	Off	3K	8K	4K	6K	Off	12K
9	Off	3K	8K	4K	6K	Off	14K
10	Off	4K	8K	4K	5K	Off	16K
11	Off	4K	9K	4K	5K	Off	14K
12	Off	3K	9K	5K	6K	Off	16K
13	Off	4K	10K	4K	6K	Off	16K
14	Off	4K	10K	4K	4K	Off	18K
15	Off	4K	8K	4K	10K	Off	12K
16	Off	3K	8K	Off	4K	Off	21.1K

HALF-MARATHON SAMPLE SCHEDULE (MILES)

WEEK	MON.	TUES.	WED.	THURS.	FRI.	SAT.	SUN.
1	Off	2 miles	3 miles	2 miles	4 miles	Off	4 miles
2	Off	2 miles	4 miles	2 miles	4 miles	Off	4 miles
3	Off	2 miles	4 miles	2 miles	4 miles	Off	5 miles
4	Off	2.5 miles	4 miles	2.5 miles	4 miles	Off	5 miles
5	Off	2.5 miles	4 miles	3 miles	4 miles	Off	6 miles
6	Off	2 miles	4.5 miles	3 miles	4 miles	Off	6 miles
7	Off	2 miles	4.5 miles	3 miles	4 miles	Off	6 miles

8	Off	2 miles	5 miles	2.5 miles	4 miles	Off	7.5 miles
9	Off	2 miles	5 miles	2.5 miles	4 miles	Off	9 miles
10	Off	2.5 miles	5 miles	2.5 miles	3 miles	Off	10 miles
11	Off	2.5 miles	5.5 miles	2.5 miles	3 miles	Off	9 miles
12	Off	2 miles	5.5 miles	3 miles	4 miles	Off	10 miles
13	Off	2.5 miles	6 miles	2.5 miles	4 miles	Off	10 miles
14	Off	2.5 miles	6 miles	2.5 miles	2.5 miles	Off	11 miles
15	Off	2.5 miles	5 miles	2.5 miles	6 miles	Off	7.5 miles
16	Off	2 miles	5 miles	Off	2.5 miles	Off	21.1K miles

SAMPLE TRAINING PROGRAM FOR MARATHON

WEEK	MON.	TUES.	WED.	THURS.	FRI.	SAT.	SUN.
1	Off	6K	10K	8K	10K	Off	15K
2	Off	6K	10K	8K	10K	Off	15K
3	Off	8K	10K	6K	10K	Off	17K
4	Off	8K	10K	6K	10K	Off	17K
5	Off	6K	12K	6K	8K	Off	19K

6	Off	6K	12K	6K	8K	Off	21K
7	Off	6K	10K	8K	1K	Off	23K
8	Off	8K	10K	8K	10K	Off	26K
9	Off	8K	10K	8K	10K	Off	29K
10	Off	6K	8K	6K	10K	Off	32K
11	Off	6K	1K	8K	10K	Off	26K
12	Off	8K	12K	8K	10K	Off	23K
13	Off	6K	8K	6K	10K	Off	32K
14	Off	6K	10K	8K	10K	Off	26K
15	Off	6K	10K	8K	10K	16K	Off
16	Off	8K	10K	Off	Off	3K	42.2K

SAMPLE MARATHON SCHEDULE (MILES)

WEEK	MON.	TUES.	WED.	THURS.	FRI.	SAT.	SUN.
1	Off	4 miles	6 miles	5 miles	6 miles	Off	9 miles
2	Off	4 miles	6 miles	5 miles	6 miles	Off	9 miles
3	Off	5 miles	6 miles	4 miles	6 miles	Off	10.5 miles
4	Off	5 miles	6 miles	4 miles	6 miles	Off	10.5 miles
5	Off	4 miles	7.5 miles	4 miles	5 miles	Off	12 miles
6	Off	4 miles	7.5 miles	4 miles	5 miles	Off	13 miles

7	Off	4 miles	6 miles	4 miles	6 miles	Off	14 miles
8	Off	5 miles	6 miles	4 miles	6 miles	Off	16 miles
9	Off	5 miles	6 miles	4 miles	6 miles	Off	18 miles
10	Off	4 miles	5 miles	4 miles	6 miles	Off	20 miles
11	Off	4 miles	6 miles	4 miles	6 miles	Off	16 miles
12	Off	5 miles	7.5 miles	4 miles	6 miles	Off	14 miles
13	Off	4 miles	5 miles	4 miles	6 miles	Off	20 miles
14	Off	4 miles	4 miles	4 miles	6 miles	Off	16 miles
15	Off	4 miles	4 miles	4 miles	6 miles	10 miles	Off
16	Off	4 miles	5 miles	Off	Off	2 miles	26.2 miles

THERE'S NO SUCH THING AS JOGGING

I wish the word *jogging* could be erased from the English dictionary. I can't tell you how many times I've had people ask me, "Are you actually running, or *just* jogging?" I suppose it's the judgment implied in this question that irks me the most. People who ask this are no doubt looking for a way to diminish what you are doing in their minds. This line of thinking, I suppose, involves the belief that you are only running if you are going at a particular speed. I guess they think there is some magic pace at which you suddenly shift from being "just a jogger" to being a "real runner" worthy of respect. It is my opinion that no such magic pace exists. I believe that if you feel you are running, you are running. I believe this for a number of reasons. First of all, distance running—that is, going for any distance longer than a short sprint—requires that you run slower than you actually can. To run a marathon you must run slower than you would run a 5K race, or you would never make it to the finish line. And both would be run at a pace that is slower than you actually can run because no one can maintain her maximum pace for any longer than a few minutes (see the section on anaerobic metabolism). Therefore, all runners are usually running at a pace that is some percentage of their optimal effort. For each of us, that maximum level of effort will be different, so all of our slower paces will be different. Let's say an 18-year-old man (who never goes running) sees a 45-year-old woman "running" past him at what he would consider a very slow pace. Let's say he decides (let's hope this has never happened or ever will) to sprint past her to see just how fast he can go compared to her. And let's say he blasts past, leaving her in his dust. Now, he might just end up being one of those people who calls what she was doing "just jogging" because she wasn't going very fast compared to him. But suppose she was a marathon runner. Let's say she'd run 20 marathons, in fact. And let's say that this particular day she was going for a 35K training run in preparation for her next event—just a part of a 70K-a-week regime. She may well have been coming to the end of a three-hour-plus run that day, pacing herself, knowing what her body could take over the long haul. Who's the "real runner" now?

If you need a way to divide those who are truly committed to running from those who are not, judge the commitment, not the speed. If someone goes out on the occasional weekend for a painful 5K run when she's feeling guilty over some indulgence or making a halfhearted attempt at starting a workout schedule, perhaps she shouldn't be taken as seriously as those who hit the pavement on a regular basis. They actually call people like this "weekend warriors." While any derogatory term is distasteful to me, I do prefer any judgment of a runner's output to be based on how committed she is to the sport rather than something as unreasonable as speed.

CHAPTER SEVEN

ZONING OUT

One of my favorite running shoe ads features a female runner wearing a T-shirt that says, I'M IN A BLISSFUL, INCOHERENT DAZE. No doubt, that T-shirt was designed by someone who knew a thing or two about the trance running helps you fall into. That "daze" is a kind of stage where many of the psychological benefits of running are played out. You often need to get to that place in order to fully relax, release your tension, and clear your mind. But getting into that state is not always easy. Sometimes it's very difficult to relax enough to get into a groove. When this happens, you may end up having an uncomfortable run physically and not coming back with the full emotional release you could have. This chapter outlines a number of tips that can help you zone out to maximize the pleasure and benefits of your runs.

BREATHING IS CRUCIAL

Without a doubt, a major element of having a fun, rewarding run is getting control of your breathing. There are a number of reasons why you can lose control over your breath during a run. You may be breathing erratically or shallowly; you could be running too fast; or you may be ill or coming down with something. It could also simply be a case of not getting into a nice breathing rhythm, something that beginner runners often struggle with. In any case, it's a good idea to work out a breathing pattern that works for you. Then you can forget about how you are breathing and relax into your run. It's very difficult to let your mind wander when you feel as though you can't get enough air. The breathing pattern I like to encourage my students to follow is an "in-in, ooouuutttt" pattern. Although no one breathes in entirely through her nose, I suggest taking your air in primarily through your nose on the "in-in" counts, then out your mouth for two counts. Some people like to coordinate their breathing pattern with their foot plants, breathing in when they are off the ground, then letting the air out on a count when one of their feet has hit the ground. Everyone is going to have a different ideal breathing pattern. You need to find what works best for you. After a while, your breathing pattern will become second nature to you. However, on those days that you find it hard to zone out, concentrate again on your breathing pattern to get into that groove.

ASSOCIATION AND DISSOCIATION

For some people, the best way to have a comfortable run is to totally associate, meaning focus completely on what they are doing. They think about how their legs, feet, arms, and other body parts are moving, how fast they are going, how they are breathing—all the tiny things going on with their body along the way. This requires some real mind control and focus. To me, it sounds torturous. Meanwhile, most runners find the best way to have an enjoyable run is to *dis*associate, that is, separate yourself from what you are doing. In my opinion, this is the best way to have a good run. But it's not always easy to dissociate from what you are doing. It requires letting go of the here and now and getting to a place where you can relax. Sometimes shaking my head and rumbling my lips as I blow out helps me loosen up. Or try shaking your hands out and rolling your head.

GO SOMEPLACE IN YOUR MIND

It's also important to pick a "place" to go. By this I mean a place in your mind where you'd like to be. As I've outlined in past chapters, you can pick a topic that is upsetting you and you can go there, engulf yourself in that issue, and zone out from the reality of where you actually are. The idea is to let go of the fact that you are running on the sidewalk past the corner store you frequent and move into your mind. Perhaps there's something that you are hoping to have happen—getting a raise or winning an award or going on a date with a certain someone. Whatever it is, pick something and go there.

When I'm training for a marathon, I sometimes envision myself running across the finish line in record time with my family and friends screaming and clapping. Sometimes I move from topic to topic, filling in between "places" with little inspiring thoughts or hopes about things. This may sound a bit crazy, but it really is a big part of what makes running so relaxing. It's meditative and autohypnotic. Your thoughts are like a mantra, something you envision in your mind and focus on instead of what is happening around you in reality. And as research has shown, you do actually put yourself into a bit of a hypnotic state. You leave reality and get to pick where you are going. It happens quite naturally, too. Quite against your will, even, although sometimes it takes a bit of work. When I don't have a particularly good run it's often because I haven't successfully zoned out. I'll get frustrated and go through lots of different topics in my mind until I find something I want to think about. Sometimes I'll even punch the air in front of me if I'm upset about something or, more to the point, someone. It's a great way to get out your aggression.

Once you've zoned out, you can actually come back to reality while staying in that relaxed, detached state. For instance, I've been known to start singing to myself while running downhill. I feel like a bird. Now, that's not something I would ever be able to do at the start of a run. It's after you've gotten into your groove and feel relaxed that you can get silly like this. In this state, you couldn't be farther from your problems or life stresses.

WHEN THE GOING GETS TOUGH, ZONE OUT

While zoning out is helpful in all your runs, it can be particularly beneficial when you come across a hard part of your route or when you are racing. There's a hill at about the halfway point of the Canadian International Marathon in Toronto that is a real killer. Despite being born and raised in the Toronto area, I didn't even know Hogg's Hollow existed. So when I came upon it in my first marathon, I stopped, looked at it, and said to myself, "You've got to be kidding." A man standing at the side of the road shouted out, "It's all downhill after this," which was little consolation. I made it up that hill with a lot of walking, but when I went back to run it the next time in my third marathon, I made sure I was ready. I had learned that picking a word or phrase and chanting it in my mind (sometimes a little bit aloud, too) helped me make it through those tough points. So I chanted, "Go hoggy, go hoggy, go!" in a nice cheerleaderesque rhythm. "Go hoggy, go hoggy, go! Go hoggy, go hoggy, go!" Over and over. It worked very well.

I actually learned this technique in the New York City Marathon. I had a great race up until the last 2 miles, which are all up and down through Central Park. So I started telling myself, "Zone out, zone out." I just repeated this over and over in my head because the pain was so intense and I just wanted to stop, but I knew I couldn't. I had to keep going, so I "zoned out."

ZONE OUT, BUT BE SAFE

With all of this said, it's important to note that runners can be at risk of being crime victims because we can be so detached. This is why I suggest not wearing a portable radio headset unless you are in a populated area. Although having some of your most inspirational musical tunes pumping into your ears can be a great aid in detaching from reality, it can set you up for being completely caught off guard. You want to be able to hear someone coming up behind you. Even when you are zoned out, your ears still work. You may not be concentrating on what you hear around you, but your senses don't stop working.

LET IT BECOME SECOND NATURE

Just as with your breathing patterns, the process of zoning out becomes natural after a while. But it's important to remember a few tricks on how to get yourself into this state so that you'll be ready on those days when you just can't seem to get into it. Mastering these techniques can also mean you'll get into the zone earlier in your runs, making the best use of every minute out there on the road.

CHAPTER EIGHT

GOAL SETTING

When I started running on the spot in my bedroom 10 years ago, my goal was to eventually be able to run on the spot for more than 12 minutes. The 12-minute barrier was an important one to me because it was the length of time we had to run in high school gym class to pass the course. I was terrorized by that run. I was always one of the last girls to finish. I was one of the chubby girls, too, and it was humiliating. So once I passed 12 minutes, I was thrilled. I think I even cried. My point of telling you this story is twofold: First, no goal is too small, and second, everyone has to figure out what goal is best for her. Whether you are starting with walking and working your way up to a walk-run combo, or whether you are starting with regular runs of 5K or more, goals are an important part of what keeps us committed to becoming better runners. Goals can inspire you, keep you focused, and set out a course for you to follow. It's also pretty hard to commit to something that hasn't been defined.

SET YOUR FOCUS

It's easy to flounder when you're getting started with a new healthy lifestyle. It's natural for people to drift back to the way they normally do things. It's far more natural than changing your course. It takes a great deal of willpower and drive to pull yourself off the path you've been following and head in a new, healthier, direction. But setting a goal you can focus on, think about, plan for, tell people about . . . well, it makes it easier.

One woman I know of made herself a chart of the map of Canada. As she ran her miles each day, she would add them up and chart the distance on the map. Her goal was to eventually "run across Canada." That's a pretty hefty goal, but being able to add just a few miles to her chart each day made her feel committed to what she was doing.

START SMALL

I like to suggest to people to start off with small goals. For instance, tell yourself that you are going to do a run-walk combo you can manage three times in your first week. Or perhaps just getting out that door the first time is a more manageable goal. Whatever it is, set an immediate goal that you can work on now. It's important to be realistic about what you can do so that you don't put on more pressure than you can handle, or, worse, hurt yourself.

The next step is to set a goal for a couple of months down the line. With the run-walk programs in this book, most beginner runners will be able to run a 5K race after about 10 weeks. Go to your local running store or go online to one of the running magazines and find out what races are coming up in your neighborhood. You'd be amazed how many of these fun runs are taking place all through the year.

SET LONG-RANGE AND DREAM GOALS

Perhaps setting a long-range goal will also help inspire you to stick with your routine. Perhaps running a marathon or qualifying for the Boston Marathon is your long-range, maybe-one-day goal. I never dreamed in a million years that I'd one day have three marathons under my belt, so even if it seems too lofty to be possible, if you've thought about it, write it down. Don't forget there are 15K races, half-marathons, mini triathlons, Iron Man competitions, ultramarathons (30 miles on up), and theme marathons all around the world. Don't be afraid to dream big. You never know what you might end up doing. These dream goals can provide the romance and intrigue that running a 5K race may not. In those final, sometimes painful minutes of a training run, it's amazing what imagining yourself running across a marathon finish line to the thunderous applause of your friends and family will do for you.

RECORD YOUR GOALS

Once you've decided on a goal, it's important to record it. Write it down in a journal, in a mile log, on a calendar—whatever works best for you. Mark down what you want to do, plan how you're going to do it, and pat yourself on the back when it's done. Each time I hunker down for another four months of marathon training, I make up a schedule on post it on the fridge. I check off each run as I do it and record how it went and how long it took me to run it. It's great to be able to see how I have day by day, week by week, worked up to my goal. It's also encouraging to see how many miles are already behind me. And placing this schedule in a public place like the refrigerator makes my commitment to the plan that much greater. This way I've told my family and anyone who comes through the house that this is what I'm working toward. It's hard to back out of something when you've made a public commitment this way.

LEAVE ROOM FOR ADJUSTMENT

It's also important to monitor, evaluate, and adjust your goals depending on what happens in your life. If you've sustained an injury, it may not be feasible for you to continue with the schedule you've planned. Or maybe you've found that it just is too much for you. Don't fret. Sit down and work out a new plan. You may have to take some time off or adjust your expectations, but as long as you've set a new goal, you'll be fine.

Watch that you don't let these life troubles stop you from continuing, however. In my running clinics I've had many women tell me about problems in their lives that they felt warranted ending their training program. The truth is, even when there's been a tragedy like a death, running can actually be one of the best things for you. This may sound a little callous, but it's true. Running gives you something you can control when it seems like there's nothing you can. It gives you a chance to sort out your thoughts, get away, cry. Stick to your goal, if you can. In the end, you'll be glad you did.

WEIGHT-LOSS GOALS

I discourage people from setting goals associated specifically with weight loss. This is particularly important for runners, who gain quite a bit of muscle during a training program, which may cause them to actually gain weight while they are getting slimmer and healthier. Use the way your clothing fits as an indicator (maybe not those cotton jeans that get loose between washings!), or use a measuring tape to monitor how your body is changing. I occasionally take measurements of my thighs, hips, and waist to make sure nothing has changed too much. It's a far better indication of how you are doing with your workouts than what the scale says.

BE REALISTIC

While dream goals are great, it is important to be realistic. If you set the bar too high, you won't be able to achieve your goal. All that this will succeed in doing is causing you to feel deflated and less likely to keep with it. Not to mention the fact that you can hurt yourself. So, again, take it slow. On the other hand, if you feel after a few weeks that you really can do more, adjust your program to reflect that. Many of the beginner runners I have taught start off thinking they'll never be able to run 5K in their lives only to find they are doing it on a regular basis by the end of our 10-week program. Then they feel the 5K race they set as their goal isn't hard enough. I usually tell them to try it without walk breaks or even to pick up the pace a little bit.

Your goals should be your very own. Don't try to keep up with or stay back with anyone else who may have a different ability level than you. You shouldn't expect anything more from yourself than your own very best. If you try to compete with someone else, you'll often end up disappointed. Often runners will hook up with partners who make it easier for them to go out and do their runs each week. This is great as long as neither of you is feeling held back or pushed.

CHAPTER NINE

GEARING UP: What to Wear

CLOTHING

I felt like I was running naked the day I traded in my beloved cotton race T-shirts for a proper running top. I had proudly worn those race shirts because I wanted the world to know I was a runner. The irony was that by wearing those shirts, I was proving just how little I knew about running. Cotton is your enemy as a runner. It stays wet, gets heavy, and causes chafing—all the things you don't want in run wear. I couldn't believe the difference the day I tried out a CoolMax T for the first time. It felt so light, so free, so dry. I've never worn cotton since. But the truth about cotton is just one facet of what you'll need to know to dress right for your runs. There are a number of tricks of the trade that can make your running experience more comfortable so you can zone out, relax, and have a good run.

Cotton versus Synthetic

What makes CoolMax and other synthetic fibers ideal for athletes is the fact that these materials were designed to wick the moisture away from your body. As you sweat, the fabric (others include Dri-F.I.T., Supplex, and Ultrasensor) absorbs the moisture and pulls it to the outside of the garment, allowing it to be evaporated. While this may eventually happen with cotton, it takes much longer. You would never wear a cotton bathing suit because it would take too long to dry. Not only that, but it would also fall down from the weight all the water absorbed. Synthetic fibers don't hold moisture in the way cotton does. Another reason for keeping cotton out of your running wardrobe is the fact that it changes texture once it gets wet. It becomes rough and is an ideal agent for chafing. I learned this lesson well once after buying the cheapest running bra I could find. It was CoolMax on the inside (where it matters most) but cotton on the outside. After one long run in the bra, I came back with a ring of chafing along my chest. It seems the portion of the cotton that folded over onto my skin cut right into me. Ouch. While the proper running clothes are consistently more expensive than cotton garments, the benefits are well worth the cost. Besides, synthetic garments tend to last longer than their cotton counterparts.

Layering

The best approach to dressing for runs in cooler weather is the layering method. First comes what is called your base layer. This consists of, for example, a relatively thin but long-sleeved CoolMax top. In order to allow this layer to properly wick away moisture, you want your base layer to lie close to the skin, so don't select a loose-fitting garment for your base. The next layer is your insulating layer. An ideal insulating layer would be a fleece top. This layer should be made of a synthetic fiber, to allow the moisture drawn away by the base layer to pass through with little absorption. This layer gives you a little more warmth while allowing for breathability. Then your top layer should be a lightweight synthetic fabric that will block the wind and rain, such as a windbreaker jacket. These layers tend to be more important on the top portion of your body, as that's where you'll tend to get colder first. However, some winter running pants actually incorporate all three layers, with windbreaker material on the front. Only in very cold weather will you need all three layers, but the basic principles of layering should help you find what you'll need on cooler days. Sometimes a base layer and top layer are all that you need; other days only a base layer. It's up to you, and the weather.

Dress for the Day

When you are deciding what to wear out on a run, it's important to remember that once you start running, you will feel as though it is 20 degrees F (11 degrees C) warmer than it actually is outside. That means that you should dress for weather that is much warmer. You should feel cool when you start. If you are warm, you're wearing too much. Within 5 to 10 minutes, you will have warmed up enough that your clothing will be more than you need. Even when I run on days with windchill in the –30s, I still sweat. For that reason, I'm not a fan of Gore-Tex. It's the only material that is totally waterproof, while allowing moisture out. However, I think it provides more warmth than most runners will ever need.

Putting this gear know-how to use, let's look at some examples of what you might want to wear in different weather conditions:

- ✔ **A 60-DEGREE DAY:** You'll want to dress as though it's 80 degrees, so I suggest shorts and a T-shirt. You might want to start off with a windbreaker jacket that can be folded into itself and worn around your waist or one that at least has zippers that can open the jacket up and allow good air circulation.

- ✔ **AN 80-DEGREE DAY:** Wear as little as you can. A singlet (sleeveless top) or a bra top with shorts is all the coverage you'll need on a day like this.

- ✔ **A 30-DEGREE DAY:** Believe it or not, a base layer and light jacket with long running pants is probably all you'll need on a day this cool. Remember that it will feel like it's 50 degrees outside. But don't forget a hat and gloves.

- ✔ **WHEN IT'S 0 DEGREES:** This is when you'll want to use all three layers or even more. You can add extra layers to the base or insulating layer, depending on just how cold it is out there. Coverage of your head, hands, and ears becomes important on days like these. Smothering Vaseline on exposed skin would also be advisable for added protection from frostbite and wind.

While the basic running T-shirts, singlets, pants, and shorts work for most people, some find that certain designs cause them to chafe under their arms or between their legs. Bicycle shorts are a great alternative for those who find looser shorts cause chafing. As for chafing in other areas, try out different designs to see what works best for you.

Your Feet

It's easy to forget about your feet. Since they are the body part that's taking the most abuse during your runs, you'll want to make sure they are as comfortable as possible. Synthetic socks are very important. Blisters, black toes (toenails that fall off from the pounding of running), athlete's foot, and other ailments can make running painful. You want socks intended to pull moisture away from your feet. Running socks also come in different designs that can make it less likely that you'll develop blisters or black toes. For some people, double-layered socks do the trick, while others like ultrathin socks. Most running socks also come with padding at the toes and heels, which also helps protect your feet.

Hands

Don't forget your paws! Your fingertips tend to be one of the first places to feel the cold, so remember to wear gloves or mittens on those cooler days. You can always take them off if it warms up enough. Mittens are also warmer than gloves because your fingers can help keep each other warm. Again, you don't want cotton on your hands.

Sport Bras

For women, the sport bra is essential. Not only is it uncomfortable to run without proper support, but running can actually stretch the ligaments that support our breasts, making them sag prematurely. There are two basic designs for sport bras: the compression type, which presses both breasts together and against your chest with one strip of fabric; and the encapsulation bra, which separates each breast into its own support cup. The latter is the preferred choice for women with larger breasts. While it can be hard to find the bra that suits you, it's important to shop around until you do. If you still can't find enough support, some women wear two bras on top of each other.

Avoid Infection

Aside from the reasons listed above, it's important for women to wear synthetic fibers designed for sport on the bottom because yeast infections and the fungus that causes athlete's foot love moist, warm conditions. I once developed an athlete's-foot-type fungus under my breast from going on long runs and having my sweat sit on my chest for so long. (Don't forget to change out of those sweaty clothes right after you run, too.)

Your Head

A baseball cap has become my preferred hat for running. In the summer it shields me from the sun while letting my head breathe, on rainy days it keeps the raindrops out of my eyes, and in the winter I couple it with a headband to cover my ears. With 70 percent of our body heat lost through the top of our heads, it's important to keep it covered on those cold days. But alternately, it's important to allow your head to breathe, so pick a hat made of a synthetic fabric. While you might not want to cover your head in the sun, it's an important part of staving off heatstroke. And don't forget your eyes. Sunglasses will protect your eyes from the harmful rays of the sun, keep you from being blinded temporarily be the sun and not seeing where you are going, and protect your eyes from debris flying around in the wind. They can also help slow the onset of wrinkles around the eyes, something many people who spend a lot time outside find is a problem.

Reflective Gear

If you are planning to do any of your running after dark, it's critical that you wear clothing with reflective patches. Drivers simply cannot see you in the dark. Fortunately, most athletic wear is made with elements of reflective material. If not, you can buy reflective vests, ankle strips, and stickers that let drivers see you as soon as their headlights hit you. Don't assume you are safe out there even with reflective clothing. You may see the drivers, but don't assume they can see you.

Sport Watches

By far my most valued piece of running equipment is my Nike Triax watch. I never take it off. I even wear it with evening gowns! It wasn't until I was training for my second marathon that I decided to put out the money for one. But once I had it, I regretted not investing in a sport watch sooner. With a stopwatch or chronograph function, you can keep track of the length of time you're out there; with a lap-memory function, you'll know exactly how long it took you to run a particular lap or mile; and the timer function gives you an alarm for your run-walk times. Once you've run with someone who has a watch that beeps when it's time to take a walk break and again when it's time to start running again, you'll find it hard to run without one. Some of the more advanced watches also have memory functions that can store your run times for future reference. They also have alarm-clock functions to help get you up for those early-morning runs.

Water Bottles

The water bottle is one of the most important pieces of running equipment. For runs of more than 5K or 3.1 miles, it's essential that you take along a supply of water to keep your body cool and working properly. On warm days, it's advisable to have a water bottle with you during runs of any length. So make the water bottle your friend.

Fanny Packs

The fanny pack is something that every runner should get used to wearing. While it can be uncomfortable and awkward at first, once you've been wearing one for a while, you'll forget it's there. The fanny pack is the best way to carry your money, keys, CD players, power foods, and whatever else you might need to take along. The most important function of this pack, however, is to carry the water bottle. It's best to keep your hands free while you're running, and the fanny pack allows you to do this. There are a wide variety of these carriers, everything from a simple water holder, to a water holder with a couple of small pockets, to two water holders with a CD player case and zipper pockets. It's up to you what kind of pack you'd like to carry, but remember not to load yourself up with too much stuff.

Your critical carry-on is your water; too many other things can weigh you down.

Sunscreen

Gone are the days when we could all frolic and play in the sun without protection. As runners, we spend a lot of time outside, so it's essential that we wear sunscreen to protect our skin from the harmful rays of the sun. There are lots of sunscreens made specifically for active people, that don't melt away with sweat. Also remember to pick a sunscreen with a UV rating of at least 15 and with protection from both UVA and UVB rays.

Heart Rate Monitor

Heart rate monitors are devices that fit around your rib cage, over your heart, and keep track of your heart rate while sending a signal carrying that information to a wristwatch. These devices are handy if you want to keep on top of how close you are to your maximum heart rate—for instance, in speedwork and hill training. However, I find that paying so much attention to my body stops me from being able to just zone out, so I stay away from heart rate monitors. While they are fun toys to play with, I find they are of the most benefit to those who are training for personal best (PB) times in races like the marathon and triathlons.

Distance-Measuring Devices

One way to calculate the distance you are running is with a pedometer. This device measures your distance by counting the number of times you land (it has a sensor) and multiplying that number by the length of your stride (which is preprogrammed into the pedometer). Some people dispute the accuracy of these devices and prefer to drive their route in a car to chart the distance. My favorite way of calculating the distance of my routes, however, is with map CD-ROMs. Map companies produce these disks, which allow you to point and click your way to an exact calculation of your distance. The accuracy of these CD-ROMs is amazing, allowing you to measure through parks, between creeks and buildings, and virtually everywhere you run.

Sports Baby Stroller

Just as there's no reason to stop running because you are pregnant (see chapter 17 on pregnancy), there's also no reason to stop running because you've got a child in tow. There are a number of brands of sports strollers on the market, which give runner-moms the option of taking the kids along. Offering everything from off-road-sized wheels, to diaper-bag holders, to rain covers, these strollers are lightweight and easy to take along on a run. Most also come with a safety tether-strap that can be looped around your wrist (to keep the stroller from getting away) and strong safety brakes. Many manufacturers now offer strollers built for two children. They do take up quite a bit of space on the sidewalk, however, so if you use one you might want to consider the limitations of your run route. It's also important to note that these strollers come with guidelines about how old a child must be and how much he can weigh to be safe. Usually the manufacturers of these strollers suggest a baby under the age of six months should not be placed inside due to neck muscle issues. Check your owner's manual before taking your child with you for a run. You may also want to check in with your doctor. It's a good idea to shop around before making a purchase. The quality of these strollers varies greatly. While each make must meet certain safety requirements, the level of quality can make a huge difference when it comes time to fold the strollers up for storage. I've seen many mothers taking their kids along on their runs and even on races; more often than not the children are sleeping or having fun looking around. For a mother with a small child, a sports stroller can be essential to ensuring you get out for your runs when you need them.

SHOES

During my time selling shoes in a specialty running shop, I met a number of fascinating characters. Two runners in particular stand out in my mind when I think of just how important it is to buy a good pair of running shoes. The first was an African runner who had been brought to North America to train after proving himself to be among the elite runners in his event. He told us he had never worn running shoes before and that the company sponsoring him had sent him out to find some shoes. In his country, he had always run barefoot, yet managed to stay injury-free while rising to the elite ranks. Not exactly a glowing recommendation for running shoes. Neither was the veteran woman runner who came into the store one day and told me she had always run in a basic, no-frills running shoe and she figured all the fancy versions of support shoes were just a scam. Any kind of basic shoe worked for her, and she had never been injured. "Thirty years ago we didn't have all these fancy shoes, and we managed," she said. Again, not something the shoe companies would want to announce on a billboard. However, the key here is that these two people were clearly gifted biomechanically. They didn't need special support. But most people do. If everyone who laced up and decided to start running chose to wear any old shoe without further thought, there would be a lot of injured runners giving up on the sport. There were a lot fewer runners 30 years ago than there are now. Perhaps that's partially to do with the fact that shoe companies have created shoes that can keep almost anyone healthy enough to run a lifetime.

What Foot Type Are You?

Considering the fact that you land with a force between 1.5 and 5 times your body weight each time your foot hits the ground (which is 500 to 750 times each K or 800 to 1,200 each mile), it makes sense that you'd want good cushioning from a running shoe. Many running injuries can be traced back to a bad pair of shoes, or a pair of shoes that wasn't built to support the kind of foot it's on. So to ensure that you're able to keep up with your weekly mileage, it's important to get the right shoe on your foot. Shoes are one area of your running gear that I suggest you not scrimp on.

The first thing every runner should know is that for the purpose of buying running shoes, feet are divided into three basic categories:

- ✔ **OVERPRONATORS:** Those whose feet roll in when they run.
- ✔ **SUPINATORS:** Those whose feet roll out.
- ✔ **NEUTRAL RUNNERS:** Those whose feet go through less extreme motions when they run.

A natural foot plant involves landing on the outside of your heel, then rolling onto the middle portion of your foot (while pronating, or rolling in, slightly), then pushing off the inside of the foot when you toe off. Therefore, it's natural for you to both pronate and supinate during a healthy foot plant. What is of concern, and what will likely need proper shoe support, is any excessive pronation or supination. Women tend to overpronate more than men due to the more significant angle from the hip to the knee.

The Wet Test

The best way to find out which shoe category you fall into is to go to a specialized running store and have your feet assessed by the staff. One way to do it yourself is to wet your foot and step on a piece of paper.

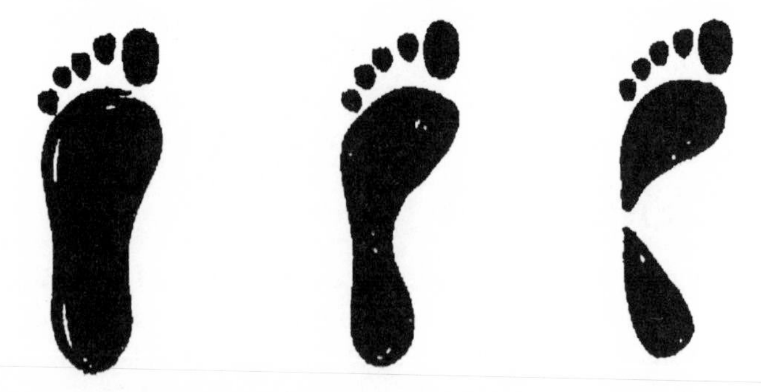

- ✔ If your footprint looks as though your entire foot touched the paper (indicating flat feet and no arch), you likely are an overpronator.
- ✔ If your footprint is S shaped, with your forefoot and heel connected by a solid arch about half the width of your foot, you likely fall into the mild overpronator or neutral category.
- ✔ If your forefoot and heel barely even connect on your footprint, or don't at all (indicating very high arches), you likely fall into the supinator category.

While this test works for most people, some flat-footed people don't actually overpronate while some high-arched people do. That's why going to a professional is ideal.

Pick Your Shoe

Once you know what category your feet fall into, you can then pick a shoe from the three main shoe categories:

- ✔ **MOTION CONTROL SHOES** are very firm, supportive shoes that help stop your foot from rolling in when you run (this category is for severe overpronators).
- ✔ **STABILITY SHOES** are not quite as firm as motion control shoes, but offer a range of support for overpronators of varying degrees.
- ✔ **CUSHIONING SHOES** provide lots of great cushioning and no corrective support. These shoes are for supinators or those with neutral feet.

Different manufacturers are known for wider or narrower shoes and provide different cushioning technologies, so it's good to try on different models within your shoe category to see what fits best for you. Feet also swell when you run, so you should make sure you have a finger-width of room at the toe.

With all these things to consider, it's easy to see why it's important not to pick a running shoe based on what it looks like or the success someone else has had with the model. By making sure you are in the proper shoe for your feet, you'll have the best chance of running injury-free.

Life of Running Shoes

Shoes last about 400 to 500 miles (800 K). A great way of knowing when your shoes are dead is when your feet start to hurt or you suddenly develop an injury. Don't let this happen, though. Keep track of your mileage so that you can have another pair of shoes broken in before you need them.

How do you know when your shoes are broken in? There is no definitive answer to that question other than to say that you will know when it happens. It's really the point at which you feel comfortable wearing the shoes, when they no longer feel brand new. It usually takes two or three 5K runs or more to work them in. It will also be during those first few runs that you will notice if anything is rubbing too much or if the shoes are too tight or too loose. Ask your shoe store about their return policy. Many times they will take the shoes back if you have only run in them indoors, on a track or treadmill. Testing them out inside, therefore, is a good idea.

Shoe-Buying Tips

- ✔ They should be finger-width at the toe.
- ✔ They should be snug in the heel.
- ✔ Buy shoes late in the day or after a run (feet swell during runs).
- ✔ Try shoes on with the socks you plan to wear.
- ✔ Bring any orthotic devices with you.
- ✔ Get advice from the person who made your orthotic on what kind of shoe you should be in to avoid getting fitted with a shoe that does the job the orthotic is supposed to do, thereby overcorrecting the problem.
- ✔ Consider the shape of your foot.
- ✔ Don't think about what it looks like.
- ✔ Don't pick based on the success others have had.
- ✔ Get a video gait analysis if possible.
- ✔ Have friends watch you run for any irregularities.

Anatomy of a Running Shoe

- ✔ **TOE BOX:** The area covering your toes at the front of the shoe.
- ✔ **HEEL COUNTER:** The firm cup at the back of the shoe that hugs the heel.
- ✔ **UPPER:** The soft material that covers the top of the shoe.
- ✔ **OUTSOLE:** The thin layer of rubber covering the very bottom of the shoe.
- ✔ **MIDSOLE:** The section of the shoe between the outsole and your foot that provides cushioning and stability support.

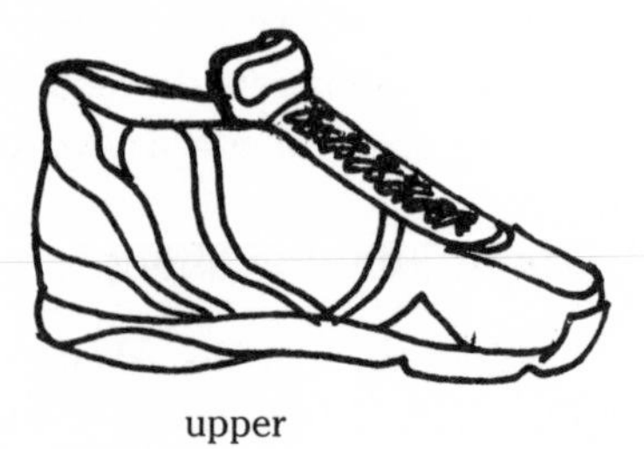

upper

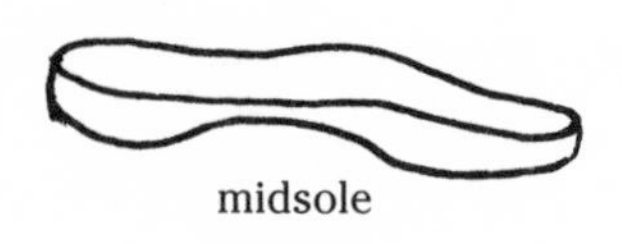

midsole

motion-control device

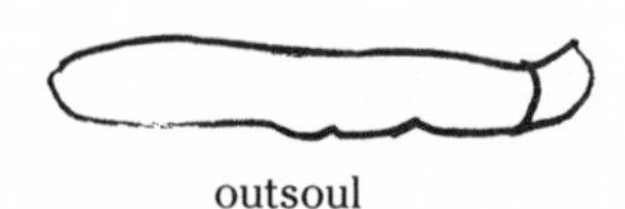

outsoul

- ✔ **MOTION CONTROL DEVICES:** Devices inserted into the midsole of the shoe to support the foot to stop overpronation. Examples include roll bars, medial posts, and footbridges.
- ✔ **LAST:** This term refers to the shape of the shoe, which can be straight, a semicurved , or curved (for high arches).

Make the Investment

If you were going to invest in only one piece of running equipment, I suggest it be a good pair of shoes, made for your kind of feet. You can usually pick up a good pair for about $100. The rest of the running gear outlined here make nice additions, but none is as necessary as what you put on your feet. Because of the technology involved and —let's face it—the fashion popularity of these outfits, running clothes can be a bit costly. You might want to do what I did—buy a piece here and a piece there until over time you've accumulated a running wardrobe. However, I must warn you, once you've run in proper running gear, you may have a hard time going back to your cotton sweats.

CHAPTER TEN

STRETCHING AND YOGA

To stretch or not to stretch, that is the question. There's been a lot of controversy about whether or not stretching improves athletic performance or provides protection from injury. Scientific studies have failed to prove that there is any significant benefit to stretching, but most fitness experts agree it is an essential part of the overall fitness continuum. Stretching gives you long, supple muscles, which may in fact contribute to stronger running performance. Aerobic fitness and strength alone are not enough. An essential element of good fitness requires you to have a full range of motion in all of your major muscle groups. Doing stretches as a part of your warm-up routine may also help protect muscles from tearing by warming them up before you make any sudden movements during exercise. Stretching can help ease the body between rest and exercise, then back to rest after the workout. It can help your body flush away lactic acid, a by-product of exercise, which can pool up in your muscles and later cause stiffness and aches. Specific stretches can also help align damaged tissue and break down scar tissue, which can aid in the injury healing process. So while stretching may not be the miracle injury prophylactic it was once thought to be, it can be a beneficial addition to your fitness routine.

As for the emotional health benefits of stretching, sitting on the ground and taking some time out of your day to loosen up your muscles is a great way to relax. Stretching diminishes the tension in your muscles and helps you let go of your worries. Not only can it warm up your body for your run, but it can get you mentally prepared to head out that door while making the start of your run a little easier physically. Stretching also makes it easier for you to get up off the floor, out of cars, and out of bed by minimizing the stiffness that can make these tasks harder than they need to be. Having greater control of your body this way can be a bit of a boost to your self-esteem. When we have trouble doing these things, we tend to feel old and weak. Stretching can help change this. Your stretching time is also a calm time, another time to relax, a time for you.

RUNNERS AND STRETCHING

Runners are notoriously inflexible. Our quadriceps, hamstrings, and calf muscles do most of our work for us when we run and tend to tighten up rather quickly. If we don't release this tension, these muscles will only get tighter, giving us very poor range of motion. A good test of just how long your muscles are is to try to touch your toes while sitting on the floor with your legs straight out in front of you. More often than not, runners can barely touch their toes, if at all. After a series of stretches for your hamstrings, however, you will be able to reach farther and farther each time. Having long muscles can help our running performance by allowing us to slightly lengthen our stride, making us faster runners.

HOW TO STRETCH

While sports medicine experts have found very little difference between those who stretch and those who don't in terms of injury occurrence, they do know that those who stretch only occasionally have the highest rates of injury. They believe sporadic stretchers stretch the wrong way and at the wrong times. It's important, therefore, to learn how and when to stretch properly.

Stretches should be done slowly, without bouncing. Stretch to the point where you feel a slight, easy stretch, but not pain. You should hold the stretch for at least 30 seconds, because the muscle will resist for the first 20. It's best to warm up your muscles before stretching. You might want to do some walking or a bit of a light run beforehand. Stretching pre-run is a good idea, but if you are going to stretch only once, doing so after your run is the way to go. As you hold the stretch, the feeling of tension should diminish. For further benefit, you can move into what is called a developmental stretch, which means moving a fraction of an inch farther into the stretch after your initial stretch to increase the tension. This kind of stretch will further improve your flexibility. Your breathing should be regular during the stretch; don't hold your breath. And don't worry about how far you can stretch. Going slowly each time will allow you to go farther each time without hurting yourself.

Stretching Tips

- ✔ Save time by stretching in the shower.
- ✔ Stay relaxed.
- ✔ Don't worry about how far you go.
- ✔ Remember to breathe.
- ✔ Stretches should feel comfortable.

TYPES OF STRETCHING

Static stretching is the most common form. It involves holding stretches for 12 seconds or longer. Some experts, however, say this kind of stretching can cause tears in the muscles, which can make the muscles ache later on. These people argue that this form of stretching is ineffective because the tendon fights the stretch after two seconds, so there's no point in doing it longer than that. They are proponents of something called active isolated stretching, which involves holding stretches for only a few seconds at a time. With this kind of stretching, however, you need to do a number of repeats, which can be time consuming.

Ideally, you should do all of the following stretches before and after you exercise—but most runners stick with the few major muscle groups and typical problem areas. Your hamstrings, calves, and quadriceps are the key muscles groups. Many runners soon learn that they need to focus on problem areas as well. These typically include the iliotibial band, the buttocks, and the nemius (because it runs into the Achilles tendon).

STRETCHES FOR RUNNERS

Calf Stretch

There are two key muscles in the back of your lower leg that need to be stretched out on a regular basis. The gastrocnemius is the large, heavy muscle below the back of your knee, and the soleus is the lower part of your calf above the heel.

Standing with your hands on the wall, bend one leg while placing the other leg straight back with your foot flat on the ground. Try to press your heel down to the ground. This stretch will target your gastrocnemius. Then, to stretch your soleus, bend the knee of your extended leg.

Iliotibial Band Stretches

While the ITB is a nonelastic band of tissue, you can actually stretch the five muscles this band of connective tissue inserts into. There are three good ways to stretch these areas. The first involves standing about arm distance from the wall. With your hand on the wall, standing up tall, cross your outside leg over your inside leg, then lean into the wall.

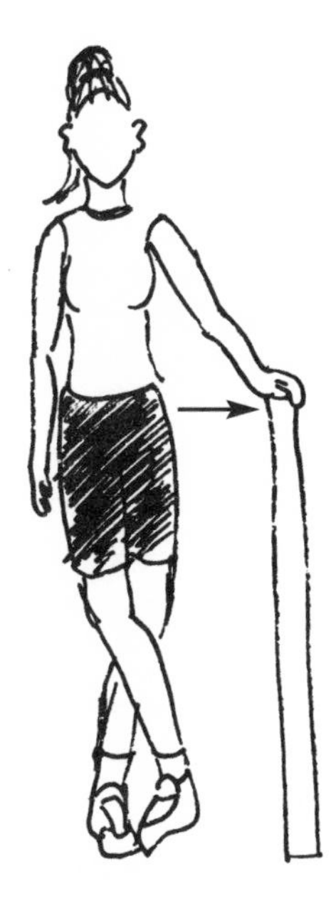

The next stretch is done sitting on the ground. With your legs bent in front of you, place your right knee over your left. Then, using your right leg, pull your left leg toward the right side of your body. Repeat on the other side.

Another way to stretch your ITB is to sit in a chair and place the foot of the leg you want to stretch on the knee of your other leg. With your hands out in front of you, lean forward. Repeat with the other leg.

Hamstring Stretches

There are two key ways to stretch your hamstrings. The first is done sitting on the ground, with your legs straight out in front of you, yet separated by about 2 feet. Bending at your hips, turn and reach for your toes. It's important to make sure you are bending at your hips and not in the middle of your back.

This stretch can also be done by placing your leg up onto a surface about 2 or 3 feet from the ground. Again bending at your hips, reach for your toes. You can bring your calves into the stretch by flexing your foot.

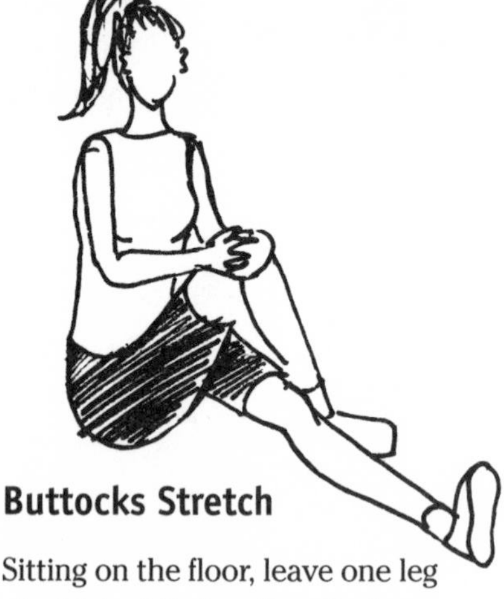

Buttocks Stretch

Sitting on the floor, leave one leg straight while bending the knee of your other leg. Cross the bent leg over the straight one, then pull your knee toward your body.

Quadriceps Stretch

Holding on to a support for balance, bend your knee and hold your foot behind your back with the hand on that same side of your body. Remember to stand up tall, keeping your hips forward. Don't lean forward or let your leg stick out to the side. Try to keep your body tall and in line.

Hip Flexor Stretch

With one knee bent on the ground, sit up on your other knee and lean forward. It's a good idea to place a pillow under your knee or do this stretch on grass or another soft surface. Repeat on the other side.

Groin Stretch

Sitting on the ground with your knees bent and feet bottom to bottom, use your elbows to gently press down on your knees. You should feel the stretch up through the inner portion of the opposite leg. Repeat on the other side.

Shin Stretch

Sitting with your feet under your buttocks, sit up tall and lean back. Some people need to nearly lie back flat on the ground to feel the stretch down the front of their shins.

Arm Stretch

With one hand against the wall at arm's length, turn your body in the opposite direction. Repeat on the other side.

STRETCHING AND LACTIC ACID

If you don't stretch after your runs, the pain you feel the day or two after that workout will be greater. Stretching and doing some body massage can help flush away the lactic acid formed during your workout. This by-product of exercise sits in your muscles and makes you feel achy a day or two after your workout. You can even feel the benefits of flushing the lactic acid out during your run, depending on how far you go. During my first marathon, my legs were so filled with lactic acid 10K from the finish that I wasn't sure I was going to make it. I stopped to stretch out my quads (with the help of another runner, who was having trouble standing on one leg herself at that point) and immediately felt better.

WARM-UPS AND COOL-DOWNS

While it's not always possible, it's a good idea to do a bit of a warm-up, of about 5 to 10 minutes, before you start into your runs. A warm-up might consist of walking slowly, then a bit faster. You may even want to jog lightly on the spot for a few minutes. Warm-ups prepare your heart, lungs, and muscles for exercise. And on the other side of your run, it's important not to sit down and stretch right after a run. You want to cool down a bit first. A cool-down can consist of simply walking for a few minutes or spending 5 to 10 minutes lightly running. If you don't take the time to cool down, your blood could pool in your muscles, causing dizziness or nausea. Cool-downs help your body make the transition back to rest.

YOGA

Yoga is not only a great complement to your running, loosening up your muscles and strengthening your weak points, but it continues that relaxing breathing you've learned in running. At the end of my two-hour yoga classes I would be lying on the ground in the fetal position, on the verge of deep sleep. It's like naptime in preschool. Next to running, yoga is the most calming thing I have ever done. Limb by limb, muscle by muscle, yoga sessions force your body to relax until you feel like a pile of mush. Happy mush.

The emotional health benefits of yoga were underscored by a study published in the *Indian Journal of Physiology and Pharmacology* in January 2001. The researchers studied 54 people between the ages of 20 and 25. Half of the group participated in yoga for 10 months, while the other half did not. The researchers found that practicing yoga reduced anxiety and depression and improved mental function. With its rhythmic breathing, meditative nature, and ability to increase blood flow, yoga can help calm the mind and body much the way running can.

While some say yoga can actually be a detriment to runners because it takes away that spring from the muscle that competitive athletes may want, I recommend it to anyone looking at running 5Ks to marathons without too much concern for a finishing time. Most of us are not competitive athletes and are just looking for some injury-free runs and a stress release.

The Sun Salutation

The five disciplines of yoga are proper exercise, yogic breathing, proper relaxation, a vegetarian diet, and meditation. While I think the yoga way of life is a wonderful path, I have not been successful in sticking with all the elements myself. I do, however, try to incorporate some yogic practices into my daily life. Some of the yoga positions and breathing exercises are very helpful in relaxing me. One element of yoga practice that I find particularly helpful is the Sun Salutation. This salutation is a series of 12 basic yoga poses performed together in flowing movements and synchronized with breath.

The Sun Salutation is a great way to start the day, get warmed up for a run, or take a time-out when things get overwhelming. The series of postures help you relax physically, but it's the breathing sequence that really lets you calm down. It gets your blood flowing and gets you limbered up for whatever you're set to do next. It also strengthens a number of muscles, including your arms and pecs—something you don't realize until a day or two after you first do it. If I'm stuck in the office (I work at home) and feeling particularly tense, but can't go for a run, I'll take a few minutes and just do a few repeats of the series.

Position One: Inhale, then exhale

Position Two: Inhale

Position Three: Exhale

Position Four: Inhale as you stretch the right leg back as far as possible, and drop the right knee to the floor. (On the next sequence you will stretch the left leg back.)

Position Five:
Exhale as you slide
into position six.

Position Six:
Bend the knees and
place the knees,
chest and forehead
on the floor.

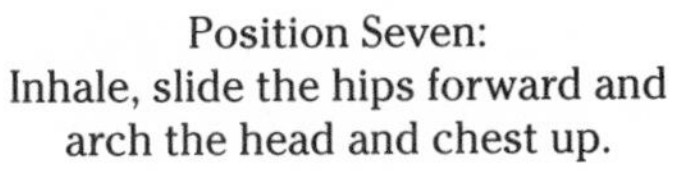

Position Seven:
Inhale, slide the hips forward and
arch the head and chest up.

Position Eight:
Exhale

Position Ten:
Exhale

Position Eleven:
Inhale as you arch back, keep arms parallel to head.

Position Twelve:
Exhale

By the time I've done two or three, I feel remarkably better. Just getting your body into a different place, getting that blood pumping and some chemicals moving, you can dramatically change your state of mind. You may not work in an environment that is conducive to dropping to the ground and doing six Sun Salutations beside your desk, but perhaps there's some room in the bathroom or a green space nearby that you could head over to on your break or lunch. Even just doing some neck and shoulder rolls at your desk, stretching your arms into the air, and doing some waist bends can help you feel refreshed.

Yogic Back Stretch (The Plow)

One of the most relaxing stretches I have found is something called the Plow. Lying on your back, kick your legs up over your head. You can hold on to your legs, keeping them straight, and work up to touching your toes to the ground behind your head. This stretches out your whole back and down the back of your legs. I like to roll from side to side while in this position because it massages all those tense back muscles. It's a great way to give yourself a back massage when there's no one around (or willing) to do it for you! Once I find one of those knots in my upper back, I hold my position, pressing my body on that point. In time, the knot diminishes in size. By the time I'm done, I feel a lot less tense.

YOGIC BREATHING EXERCISES

Yoga also provides a number of breathing sequences that on their own can be extremely calming. With your eyes closed, hold your thumb and pointer finger of your right hand over your nostrils. Pressing your thumb against your right nostril, breathe in from your left nostril for a slow count of five seconds. Then pinch both nostrils and hold that breath for another five seconds. Releasing your thumb now from your nostril, release that breath slowly to another count of five seconds. Then take in a breath from your right nostril to a count of five seconds and repeat the sequence as before. You can do as many repeats of this breathing sequence as you want. This is something you can do anywhere. If it all becomes too much in the office, just lock yourself inside a bathroom stall and take a few minutes to gather yourself with these exercises. The difference is amazing. This technique can help you get centered in the middle of the day when you can't just dash out the door for a run.

CHAPTER ELEVEN

Weight Loss and Food

Women and food. It's one of the most written about love-hate relationships of our time. Sadly, for many women, eating is not just about nourishing our bodies. In fact, for too many of us nourishment is the last thing food is about. Often, we use food to comfort us when we are low, only to feel guilty later, then suffer lowered self-esteem when it shows up on our thighs. We make food our friend, our reward, our punishment, a way to take control. The significance of food too often goes far beyond its caloric and nutrient content. We need it to survive, yet so many of us are tortured by what to eat, how much, how often. In a society where our value is often judged by how closely our bodies resemble an ultrathin ideal, we clamor to hear about the newest diets, workouts, appetite suppressants, and the like. Meanwhile, North America has become a continent of overweight people, with obesity a growing concern. A 1999 Melpomene Institute study found that nutrition was women's number one health concern, with emotional health ranking second, and weight and eating issues ranked third. Sadly, our societal value, and ultimately our self-esteem, is inextricably tied with what we look like. I make no bones about the fact that this is the very reason why I took up running. I wanted to bring my body into a healthy weight range and get some control over what I was eating. I didn't want to eat a whole large bag of potato chips on my own ever again. No doubt, many of you have taken up running to take similar control over your body and mind. While I don't advocate anyone using running to get your body to the size of a supermodel (who is typically 23 percent thinner than the average woman), running can help us feel more in control of our bodies. It can help us be healthy women, of healthy weights, with a healthier relationship with food.

MAKING THAT CHANGE

The emotional health benefits of adding running to your life are often first seen when the fat starts to melt away and those long, lean muscles start peeking through. Burning as much as 600 calories an hour, running offers a workout few other sports can. But no matter how much running you do, if you aren't eating properly, you may be canceling out all the running you are doing. Oprah Winfrey is a classic, and self-professed, example of that. She goes for 10-mile-plus training runs on the weekend and runs regularly, but has trouble keeping her weight down because of the number of calories she consumes. She may be working out as much as she ever has in her life, but it won't do as much good as it can if she simply eats more at the same time. Running is one of the fastest, most efficient ways of burning calories, but if you raise the number of calories you are eating, you won't lose weight and can in fact gain weight. To ensure you are making the most of your runs, it's important to follow some healthy eating patterns. Noted sports nutritionist Nancy Clark, author of the *Sports Nutrition Guidebook*, advocates a diet that includes a variety of foods and embraces wholesomeness and moderation. She suggests we choose low-fat options, eat lots of veggies, fruits, and grains, restrict sugar and salt, and drink alcohol in moderation. But there's lots more to know about healthy eating. Calories, Body Mass Index, fat, low-carbohydrate diets, iron deficiencies, and an array of other topics and concerns are outlined in this chapter to help you wade through the murky waters of what way is the right way to eat.

THE FAT-BURNING ZONE

To make the most of your runs, you'll want to make sure your cardiovascular system is in the right zone. Fat burning happens at the greatest rate at the bottom of the aerobic training zone, meaning when you are at about 60 to 70 percent of your maximum heart rate. The easiest way to know if you are in this zone is to do the talk test—make sure you can carry on a conversation during your run. That will let you know that you are in the aerobic zone. But if you want to be more scientific about it, you calculate your maximum heart rate by taking the number 226 and subtracting your age. If you are a particularly fit person, you should use 210 minus your age. Men should use 220. You then calculate what 60 to 70 percent of that number is and try to keep your heart beating that number of times in a minute. If you run beyond that intensity, you will be burning less fat than you could be if you just slowed it down a little. We always burn a combination of fat and carbohydrates, but as your intensity increases, the ratio turns over to burn more carbohydrates and less fat. Burning any energy is good, but when you want to lose those unwanted pounds, you want to stay in the lower end of the aerobic training zone. That zone goes up to 85 percent of your maximum heart rate, where you then move into the anaerobic zone.

BODY MASS INDEX—YOUR IDEAL WEIGHT

What the scale says we weigh is not the best indication of how close we are to what is healthy. Our height, body type, bone structure, and genetics all work together to make every person completely different. Therefore, everyone has a different ideal body weight range. The most widely accepted indicator of your ideal weight range is the Body Mass Index (BMI), created by the American Dietetic Association (ADA). The BMI allows you to calculate your ideal body mass range. Readings between 19 and 25 are considered acceptable; lower than 19 is considered too thin. Readings of 25 and above indicate a person is getting into an unhealthy weight range.

Meanwhile, in 1995, the Dietary Guidelines Advisory Committee on the Dietary Guidelines for Americans released the most updated chart on ideal weight ranges based on height. Using both charts as guides, you should be able to determine what range is best for you.

HOW TO GAUGE YOUR HEALTHY WEIGHT

Body Mass Index	19	20	21	22	20	24	25	26	27	28	29	30	35	40
Height (inches)	Body weight (pounds)													
58	91	96	100	105	110	115	119	124	129	134	138	143	167	191
59	94	99	104	109	114	119	124	128	133	138	143	148	173	198
60	97	102	107	112	118	123	128	133	138	143	148	153	179	204
61	100	106	111	116	122	127	132	137	143	148	153	158	185	211
62	104	109	115	120	126	131	136	142	147	153	158	164	191	218
63	107	113	118	124	130	135	141	146	152	158	163	169	197	225
64	110	116	122	128	134	140	145	151	157	163	169	174	204	232
65	114	120	126	132	138	144	150	156	162	168	174	180	210	240
66	118	124	130	136	142	148	155	161	167	173	179	186	216	247
67	121	127	134	140	146	153	159	166	172	178	185	191	223	255
68	125	131	138	144	151	158	164	171	177	184	190	197	230	262
69	128	135	142	149	155	162	169	176	182	189	196	203	236	270
70	132	139	146	153	160	167	174	181	188	195	202	207	243	278
71	136	143	150	157	165	172	179	186	193	200	208	215	250	286
72	140	147	154	162	169	177	184	191	199	206	213	221	258	294

The Bodywise Woman, Lutter, J., and L. Jaffee (Champaign, IL: Human Kinetics, 1996), p. 60.

CALORIES AND WEIGHT LOSS

Fat-burning zones, fat content, and low-carbohydrate diets aside, the bottom line in gaining or losing weight is the number of calories you ingest in a day. More to the point, the ultimate indicator of your weight will be the number of calories you ingest each day on a regular basis. To gain weight, you eat more calories than you can burn. To lose weight, eat fewer calories than you burn. And to remain the same weight, consume the number of calories you need. It's really quite simple.

According to Claire Kowalchik, author of *The Complete Book of Running for Women*, to lose 1 pound of fat, you will need to burn 3,500 calories. The ideal rate of weight loss is about 1 pound per week. Therefore, to lose 1 pound a week, you will need to burn about 3,500 extra calories each week, or about 500 calories each day. That could involve cutting out 500 calories you would normally have consumed, working out until you burn that amount, or some combination of both, which is the preferred route.

Running is one of the best ways to burn calories fast. Depending on how fast you are running, you will burn about 600 calories per hour. That's about 100 calories every 10 minutes. The faster you run, the more calories you will burn. Likewise, the slower you run, the fewer calories you will burn. Lifting weights can help you burn more calories because muscle burns fat. Exercise also increases your rate of metabolism (which is the measure of how quickly you are using calories). That said, you shouldn't be restricted to fewer than 1,200 calories each day. Starving yourself in the name of being thin is a losing battle because your body's metabolism will slow down to protect itself —not to mention the potentially fatal side effects that come with de-

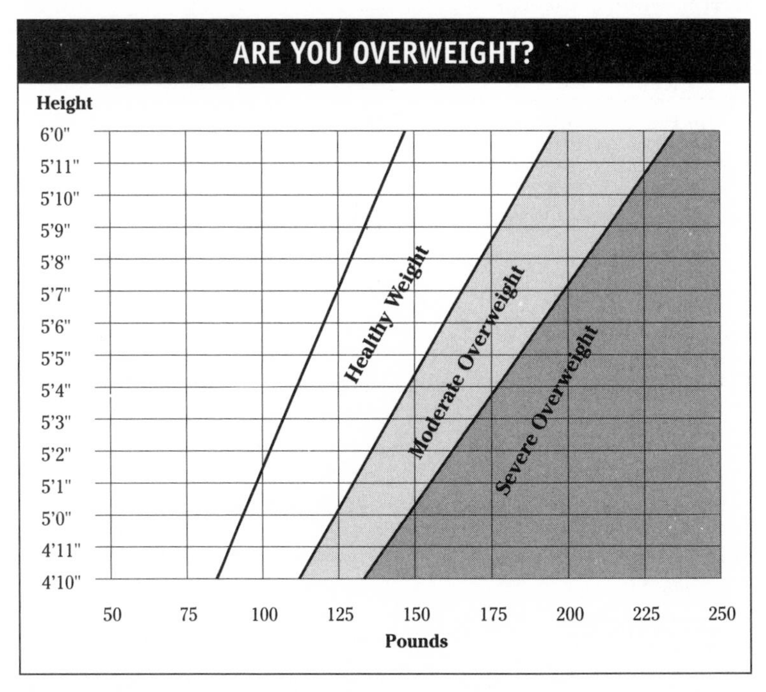

Report of the Dietary Guidelines Advisory committee on the Dietary Guidelines for American, 1995.

veloping an eating disorder. At the same time, too much exercise can be bad for you as well. Balance is the key.

While the fat content, wholesomeness, and makeup of foods can contribute to how likely that food is to put unwanted weight on you (as I'll discuss later in this chapter), don't forget to look at the bottom-line calorie content in foods. Just because something is low in fat doesn't mean that it won't cause you to gain weight. People often make the mistake of thinking they can eat all the low-fat foods they want; meanwhile, these foods could be causing you to gain weight. Make sure you know how many calories are in the food you eat.

You can cut out those extra calories and fat easily by making a few healthier choices. The chart below gives examples of some smarter choices without compromising on taste or having to starve yourself. Making just a few substitutions at the grocery store can make a world of difference to your daily calories, fat content count, and the overall wholesomeness of your diet.

Sample Choices	Healthier Choices
Butter (5 ml/1 tsp.) = 36 cal, 4 g fat	Nonhydrogenated, low-fat spread (2 tsp./10 g) = 25 cal, 2.6 g fat
2% milk (250 ml/1 cup) = 128 cal, 5 g fat	Skim milk (250 ml/1 cup) = 90 cal, trace elements of fat
Ice cream (125 ml/1/2 cup) = 142 cal, 8 g fat	Yogurt, plain (1.5 % , 125 ml/1/2 cup) = 79 cal, 2 g fat
Cheddar cheese (45 gm/1.5 oz) = 181 cal, 15 g fat	Low-fat cheddar slices (1 slice) = 51 cal, 2.9 g fat
Sour cream (15 ml/1 tbsp.) = 23 cal, 3 g fat	No-fat sour cream (30 ml/2 tbsp.) = 22 cal, 0.4 g fat
Mayonnaise (15 ml/1 tbsp.) = 100 cal, 11 g fat	Low-fat mayonnaise (15 ml/1 tbsp.) = 50 cal, 5.1 g fat
Salad dressing, French (15 ml/1 tbsp.) = 64 cal, 6 g fat	Fat-free salad dressing (15 ml/1 tbsp.) = 15 cal, no fat
Chicken, fried (140 gm)	Chicken breast, roasted (no skin,

= 364 cal, 18 g fat	90 gm/3 oz) = 148 cal, 3 g fat
Pork spareribs (2 med./70 gm) = 235 cal, 18 g fat	Pork, lean ham slices (90 gm/3 oz) = 130 cal, 5 g fat
Hamburger patty, regular broiled (90 gm/3 oz) = 260 calories, 19 g fat	Tuna, canned in water (90 gm/3 oz) = 143 cal, 1 g fat
Microwave popcorn (1 bag) = 200 cal, 11 g fat	Popcorn, air popped (250 ml/1 cup) = 25 cal, trace elements of fat (add low-fat spread; see above)
Apple pie (1/6 pie) = 404 cal, 18 g fat	Fig bars (2) = 100 cal, 2 g fat
Doughnut (1) = 165 cal, 8 g fat	Arrowroot cookies (2) = 58 cal, 2 g fat
Corn puffed cereal, presweetened (250 ml/1/2 cup) = 114 cal, trace fat	Oatmeal, cooked (125 ml/1/2 cup), = 77 cal, 1 g fat
Bread, white (one slice) = 76 cal, 1 g fat	Hollywood bread, thin sliced, whole wheat (1 slice) = 45 cal, 1 g fat
Large white fluffy bagel (1) = 600 cal, 6 g fat	Small, chewy bagel (1) = 200 cal, 2 g fat
Potato, french fries (10 strips) = 158 cal, 8 g fat	Potato, baked (1) = 148 cal, trace elements of fat
Chocolate chip cookies (6 cm diameter, 2) = 104 cal, 5 g fat	Orange (1) = 62 cal, trace elements of fat
Cheesecake (1/12 of 23 cm diameter cake) = 278 cal, 18 g fat	Fruit cocktail, canned (125 ml/1/2 cup) = 60 cal, trace elements of fat
Creamed corn (250 ml/1 cup)	Broccoli spears (150 ml/1 cup)

= 194 cal, 1 g fat	= 48 cal, trace elements of fat
Soda pop (1 can) = 119 cal, no fat	Diet cola (1 can) = 0 cal, no fat
Beer (340 ml/10 oz) = 145 cal, no fat	Wine, white (100 ml/3½ oz) = 77 cal, no fat
Liqueur, crème de menthe (50 ml/2 oz) = 210 cal, no fat	Tea/coffee (250 ml/1 cup) = 2 cal, no fat

FOOD PYRAMID

While there is never a shortage of diet gurus pitching a new way to eat to help you keep your weight down, the true experts agree on exactly how much of what we should all be eating in a day. Guidelines released by both the U. S. Department of Agriculture and the Health Canada are the same and are as follows:

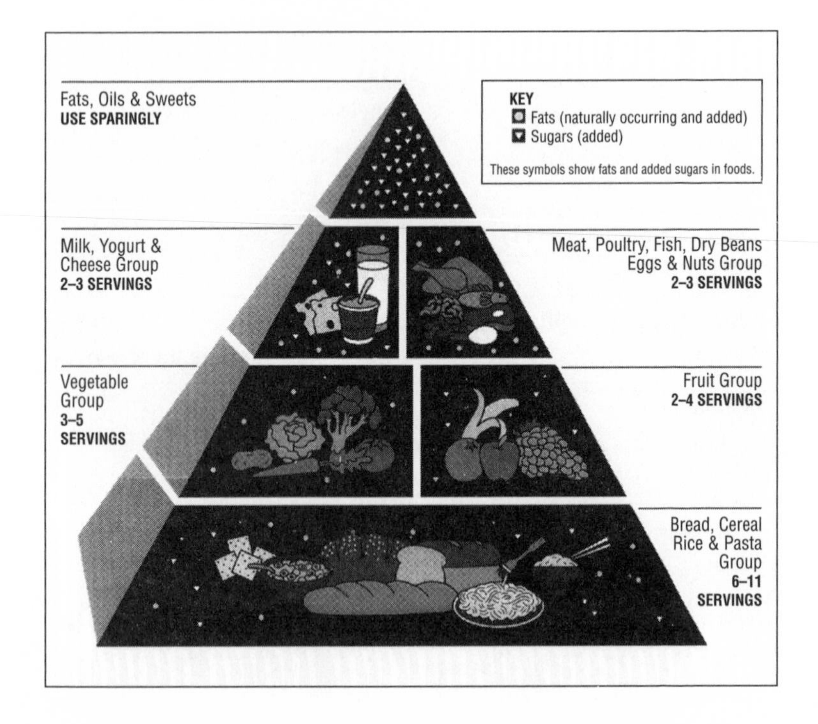

- ✔ 6–11 servings of bread, cereal, rice, and pasta
- ✔ 2–4 servings of fruit
- ✔ 3–4 servings of vegetables
- ✔ 2–3 servings of dairy
- ✔ 2–3 servings of meat and substitutes

These guidelines encourage people to eat lots of fruit and vegetables, while limiting the number of servings of the other food groups. Most people find they have a hard time keeping the number of grain and meat servings down, while they have a hard time eating enough vegetables and fruit. It can be hard to get four servings of vegetables into a day, but it's important that we try to eat enough servings in this food group and not make up the difference with, for example, more bread. Nutritionists, who know what proportions of each food group we should eat, designed these guidelines. Any diet that goes against these guidelines—suggesting we not eat fruit, for example—violates basic rules of nutrition. Sticking to these expert-approved guidelines will keep you on a healthy course.

SERVING SIZE—THE CRITICAL ELEMENT

Listening to nutritionists lecture the students of my clinics about nutrition, the one aspect of healthy eating that never ceases to amaze me is just how small serving sizes are. The American Food Guide Pyramid and the Canada Food Guide give excellent guidelines of what percentages of your diet should come from the different food groups. But these guides also specify how much of a given food constitutes a serving. You could follow the guides precisely, but if you aren't paying attention to the specifications on serving size, you could actually gain weight. Did you know that the large bagels found at most coffee shops and bagel stores count as *six* servings of bready carbohydrates? (The small, chewy— not fluffy—bagels count as two servings.) The food pyramid suggests people eat 5 to 12 servings of grain products in a given day. The 12 servings are intended for large, active men, and the 5 servings for small, less active women. If you happen to be one of those women, and you ate one of these bagels, you would have eaten one more serving of grain products than you should have had all day. And if you are a large, active man, you could have only two of those bagels in a day. That means you can't have any other bread products—cereal, rice, pasta, nothing! Hard to believe, but it's true. For most people, the number of grain servings falls somewhere in between. These serving sizes shock a lot of people, likely because people's perceptions of healthy serving sizes in North America have swelled to alarming proportions. The full plates of pasta served at many restaurants could give you more than 12 servings, since a serving of pasta is about 1/2 a cup cooked. For some people, just cutting back to proper sized servings could result in significant weight loss.

Serving Sizes

- ✔ **MEAT:** A cooked portion about the size of a deck of cards; a can of tuna; two eggs
- ✔ **DAIRY:** One cup of milk; a finger-sized piece of cheese
- ✔ **GRAIN PRODUCTS:** One slice of regular bread; 1/2 cup cooked pasta
- ✔ **FRUIT:** A banana; an apple
- ✔ **VEGETABLES:** One cup of broccoli

FOOD TYPES

To wade our way through all the fad diets on the market, and all the misconceptions about healthy eating, it's important to know some nutrition basics. The first thing we should know is that our energy comes from three sources: carbohydrates, proteins, and fats. Additionally, there are a few other nutrients our body cannot live without; they include water, vitamins, and minerals. The following section will go over each of these energy sources and nutrients, explaining why we need them, where we can get them, and how they work together.

Carbohydrates

Carbohydrates are our primary source of energy. Fruits, vegetables, and grain products all fall into this category and give us calories from sugars and starches. Carbohydrates are converted to blood glucose in our body, then stored in our muscles and liver in the form of glycogen if not used immediately. Despite all the negative attention carbohydrates have been getting in recent years (with the unfortunate popularity of the high-protein, low-carb diets), experts agree that approximately 55 to 65 percent of our total energy each day should come from carbohydrates.

While carbohydrates are essential to fueling everything we do in a day, when our carbohydrate intake exceeds our requirements they can be converted into fat and transported to the fat tissue of our bodies. So it's important to make sure you aren't eating more than you need.

SIMPLE CARBOHYDRATES Simple carbohydrates come in the form of sugars or fruits and are absorbed quickly into the bloodstream. If simple carbohydrates are taken in in large quantities, you can end up getting a sugar high, followed by a crash of low energy.

COMPLEX CARBOHYDRATES Complex carbohydrates are found in foods like bread, cereal, potatoes, pasta, and rice. They absorb into the body slowly, therefore providing a slower, steadier form of glucose. As a result, these are the kinds of foods you want to be eating a day or two before a big run or race.

BREAD, CEREAL, RICE, AND PASTA These kinds of carbohydrates are some of the favorite foods among runners. Aside from giving us the fuel to run, these foods give us needed fiber and B vitamins. It's a good idea to choose the whole-grain and enriched carbohydrates over the highly processed, fluffy white variety.

FRUITS AND VEGETABLES Fruits and vegetables are great sources of carbohydrates, fiber, vitamins C and A, and potassium. These foods help our bodies heal, can reduce our risk of developing cancer and high blood pressure, and can help keep us regular. Fruits and vegetables also contain certain antioxidant nutrients, which are believed to help reduce the risk of cancer and other diseases.

Make vegetables your friends. They are full of vitamins—including vitamin C and beta and other carotenes—potassium, and magnesium. They are water rich and yummy. There's a lot to choose from, so take your pick. I like to gorge myself on beets, carrots, and cabbage. The darker and the more colorful the vegetable, the more nutrients it has. They are also low calorie, so basically you can eat them until your heart is content.

Proteins

Protein, as the nutrient responsible for building and repairing muscles, is the building block of your body. Protein is made up of about 20 different types of amino acids. When the body needs repair—for instance, after a run—these amino acids provide the raw material. Proteins that contain all of the essential amino acids are known as complete proteins. These include foods like meat, eggs, and milk products. These complete proteins can be high in saturated fats, however, so it's important to eat them in moderation. The other kind of protein is called the incomplete proteins. They include foods like cereals, legumes, and nuts.

Protein should make up about 10 to 15 percent of your daily intake. Protein also helps reduce the risk of iron deficiency and anemia. The best choices for protein are fish and poultry because they are low in saturated fat. Excess protein not needed by the body is easily turned to fat, so it's important to make sure you are not eating too much.

Interesting fact: The average North American eats more than three times as much protein as she needs each day.

DAIRY PRODUCTS Milk, cheese, yogurt, and the like all provide the body with needed calcium, protein, and riboflavin. These nutrients help maintain strong bones, reduce risk of osteoporosis, and protect against high blood pressure. However, it is important to choose low-fat varieties of these foods because they tend to be high in saturated fats. Some of the best nondairy sources of these nutrients include tofu, spinach, soy products, and sardines.

MEATS AND ALTERNATIVES While some meats can be rather fatty, eating healthily doesn't require cutting this food group out of your diet.

Meats give us needed amino acids, which are critical to building and repairing muscles. This food group also helps us keep our iron levels in a healthy zone. Choosing less fatty varieties of meats can help you keep your fat content to a minimum while being able to enjoy your favorite meals. While the occasional steak is no problem, some of the best choices from this food group include fish, tofu, and tuna.

Fats

Fat has become a dirty word. While a healthy diet includes limiting your fat intake, fats should actually make up about 30 percent of the food you eat each day. Fat is the energy source used to fuel long-term activity, like running. That doesn't mean you should feel free to eat a lot of fatty foods.

There are good fats, or unsaturated fats, and there are bad fats, or saturated fats. Saturated fats are found in foods like cheese, butter, meat, and poultry. In many cases you will know saturated fats when you see them because they are solid at room temperature, then get runny when they are warmed up. Unsaturated fats are found in plant sources. There are two types of unsaturated fats, monounsaturated (found in olive oil, canola, peanut oil, and avocados) and polyunsaturated fats, which are found in salmon, tuna, and sardines (these are really good for you). Fats are an important component of nutrition not only because they provide needed energy, but also because they make food taste good and make you feel full. They also help in the transportation of fat-soluble vitamins like A, D, E, and K, and provide essential fatty acids. It's a good idea to choose unsaturated vegetable fats like olive oil, corn oil, or other fat sources like walnuts.

Water

With up to 75 percent of our body weight made up of water, it's easy to see why keeping our bodies well hydrated is critical. Water carries nutrients to our cells, helps flush away metabolic waste from cells, and helps regulate our body temperature. It also helps keep our skin clear, lubricates our joints, and cushions our organs and body tissues. We lose 2 liters (2 quarts) of fluid naturally each day, so it's important to keep replenishing our body's supply. We should all be drinking 8 to 10, 8-ounce glasses of water each day. But for runners it's important to top this up by drinking before our runs, during our runs, and after. You should be drinking 2 cups two hours before exercise, 1 to 2 cups in the hour leading up to your run, 1/3 to 1 cup at 15- to 20-minute intervals during exercise, and 1 cup 10 to 15 minutes after exercise.

Vitamins

Vitamins and minerals are important for our body's growth and cellular function. Essential vitamins like A, B, C, D, E, and K control the chemical reactions in our bodies and impact on our fuel pathways. We need them to function. You may not need to supplement your diet with a multivitamin if you are eating a balanced diet with lots of fruits and veggies, and the appropriate portions of meat and daily products. One exception is iron (see the section on iron deficiency).

Minerals

Like vitamins, minerals impact on our fuel pathways. Key minerals include calcium, iron, potassium, and sodium. We lose a lot of these minerals when we sweat, so it's important to make sure that your mineral levels do not get depleted. You can get lightheaded and weak when your mineral levels, or your electrolytes, get depleted. Sports drinks like Gatorade can help you replenish your stores of potassium and sodium. Bananas or salty treats can do the same.

All the Extras

Caffeine should be ingested in moderation, particularly for those who have trouble with depression, stress, anxiety, or PMS. Caffeine chemically induces our fight-or-flight response, which puts us on edge. It also dehydrates us, which is something you want to avoid as a runner. I'm lost without my 2 cups of tea in the morning, but I am careful to switch to decaffeinated later in the day and I make sure I top up my water stores to make up for the dehydrating effect of the caffeine. Caffeinated beverages include tea, coffee, and diet and regular colas.

Alcohol is another beverage that runners and those struggling with their emotional health should use in moderation. Acting as a depressant, alcohol can bring an already low mood down even farther or make you feel low even when you were feeling fine. Like caffeine, alcohol also dehydrates you. Getting up to go for a run after a night of drinking will always prove difficult unless you have made sure you rehydrated and replenished those vitamins and minerals that you lost to urination.

The third evil is sugar. As we all know, it can be found in everything from cookies to candy to cola. All foods made up primarily of sugar should be consumed in moderation. They are high in calories and will give you only a short, fast boost of energy.

Ideal Foods for Runners

Apple	82 cal, 0 g fat
Apricot, dried (10 halves)	83 calories, 0 g fat
Banana	106 calories, 0 g fat
Cantaloupe (1/2)	93 calories, 0 g fat
Orange juice (250 ml/1 cup)	118 calories, 0 g fat
Peach	37 calories, 0 g fat
Strawberries (250 ml/1 cup)	47 calories, 0.6 g fat
Fruit cocktail (125 ml/1/2 cup)	60 calories, trace fat
Broccoli (250 ml/1 cup)	48 calories, trace fat
Carrot (1 raw)	31 calories, trace fat
Mushrooms (250 ml/1 cup)	40 calories, trace fat
Potato (1 baked)	148 calories, trace fat
Squash, winter, cooked (250 ml/1 cup)	75 calories, 1 g fat
Tomatoes (1 medium)	23 calories, trace fat
Mixed vegetables (250 ml/1 cup)	102 calories, trace fat
Bran cereal (125 ml/1/2 cup)	90 calories, 1 g fat
Oatmeal (125 ml/1/2 cup)	77 calories, 1 g fat
Rye bread (1 slice)	61 calories, trace fat

Whole-wheat bread (1 slice)	61 calories, trace fat
Small bagel	200 calories, 2 g fat
Brown rice (250 ml/1 cup)	214 calories, 1 g fat
Whole-wheat pasta (3 oz.)	300 calories, 1.2 g fat
Tuna (90 g/3 oz)	143 calories, 1 g fat
Chicken breast, roasted (90 g/3 oz)	148 calories, 3 g fat
Turkey, roasted dark meat (90 g/3 oz)	161 calories, 6 g fat
Egg (1)	75 calories, 5 g fat
Red kidney beans (250 ml/1 cup)	230 calories, trace fat
Lentils, cooked (250 ml/1 cup)	244 calories, 1 g fat
Tofu (90 g/3 oz)	68 calories, 4 g fat
Skim milk (250 ml/1 cup)	90 calories, trace fat
Yogurt, plain (125 ml/1/2 cup)	79 calories, 2 g fat
Cottage cheese, 2% (125 ml/1/2 cup)	107 calories, 2 g fat
Mozzarella cheese, part skim (45 g/1.5 oz)	118 calories, 7 g fat

THE GREAT CARBOHYDRATE-VERSUS-PROTEIN DEBATE

We've all heard the stories of people going on high-protein, low-carbohydrate diets and losing tons of weight. These people eat bacon for breakfast every day and basically can indulge in anything fatty or high in protein, yet they aren't allowed to eat even one banana. These diets encourage a way of eating that is a virtual opposite of the food pyramid. All starches, sugar, grains, cereal, and potatoes are banned, while dairy products, all meats, and green vegetables are allowed. These diets, in some cases, have shown to be effective in weight loss. However, dietitians report that people on these diets have experienced low energy levels, hair loss, and other alarming side effects. The long-term effects of this kind of eating are not known. The bottom line is that this way of eating is unhealthy, not to mention unsustainable over a lifetime. The idea behind these high-protein diets is based on an unproven scientific claim that insulin makes you fat. Proponents of these diets claim foods that rapidly raise your blood sugar—thereby causing your pancreas to produce insulin in great amounts—will cause you to gain weight. The health concerns aside, this is not the kind of diet that a person could stick to for her entire life. And whenever you stop, you will simply gain back the weight you have lost. I've spoken with women who are afraid to eat any fruit for fear of gaining back weight they lost. This is a shame. The key to keeping weight off is committing to a healthy way of life for life. Balance is the key here. Yes, eating too much bread can put extra weight on you, but there's no need to eat no bread at all. Eating all foods in moderation and in the portions suggested is the goal.

BUTTER OR MARGARINE?

First we were told margarine is better than butter. Then we heard that margarine can be worse for the heart than butter. Here's the scoop: Most margarines are made using an industrial process called hydrogenation. This process brings liquid fat into a semisolid state, meanwhile causing the creation of trans-fatty acids. Studies are now showing that these trans-fatty acids are as bad for your heart as saturated fats. Therefore, hydrogenated margarines are not better for you than butter. There are some margarines, however, that are made without going through this process. So if you want to go the margarine route, you should make sure the label says it is nonhydrogenated.

VEGETARIANISM

Vegetarianism is a lifestyle choice that has grown in popularity in recent years. Perhaps as an offshoot of the heightened interest in all things Eastern, more and more people have made the decision to cut animals products out of their diets. While vegans (who eat no animal products at all) and lacto-ovo vegetarians (who eat milk products and eggs) can eat healthy, well-balanced diets without breaking vegetarian rules, it can be very difficult to get all of the proper nutrients into your diet. Ensuring you get all of the protein you need means taking the time to prepare meals with meat substitutes like tofu and beans, both of which can require a lot of preparation time. During the two years I spent as a lacto-ovo vegetarian, I found that although I had good intentions, I rarely took the time to soak my beans or marinate my tofu, and subsequently, I was often hungry. I'd fill the void I felt by eating more bready carbohydrates and cheese. I didn't think this would be a problem since I wasn't eating meat. Meat, because it can be fatty, was a worse thing to be eating, I thought. But both bread and cheese are quite high in calories, so I actually ended up gaining weight during my time as a vegetarian. Also, when you are not eating enough protein, you are likely to develop iron and other mineral deficiencies, which active women are already prone to. Meat, and all protein, is what makes you feel full. So unless you are sure you can put in the time needed, going the meat-free route isn't necessarily a healthier alternative.

EATING DISORDERS

With all this talk about women, food, and exercise, it's essential that we cover the issue of eating disorders. While the majority of women no doubt have issues with food and their body image, for some women this takes on potentially lethal proportions. A friend of mine from the university now has the intellect of a six-year-old child as a result of bulimia nervosa. Obsessed with being thin, she spent three years bingeing and purging, until finally her weak little heart could take no more. She was actually running on a treadmill inside her parents' home one day when her heart just stopped. I later found out that sudden heart failure is a leading cause of death among anorexics and bulimics. Her father came upon her lifeless body a few minutes later and managed to revive her. She ended up in a coma, then a catatonic state, then slowly began learning everything again. She remembers little from her life before the incident and possesses none of the brilliant artistic ability she once had. Ironically, she is now about 40 pounds overweight. The beauty of that, however, is that with the intellect of a child, now she doesn't seem to care.

I tell you this story on the off chance it can help someone reading this who may be suffering from an eating disorder or knows someone who is. Every year thousands of women die from anorexia and bulimia. Exercise, particularly running, is very popular among those with these problems because of its calorie-burning potential. A number of times I have had women run by me who, with no exaggeration, looked like living skeletons. While I am preaching about the fabulous weight loss benefits of running, I sternly discourage anyone who has an eating disorder from following a running plan of any kind without the strict supervision of a doctor. While running can help give you back control of your body, it can also contribute to unhealthily low body weights and have very damaging effects on your organs and overall health. The front of most phone books lists phone numbers for eating disorder help. If you think you or someone you know has one of these problems, pick up the phone and ask for help.

IRON DEFICIENCY

Iron deficiency is a concern that all female runners should know about. Athletic women of childbearing age, in particular, are susceptible to having low iron counts. With our menstrual cycles each month, we lose a fair bit of iron and it's sometimes hard for the body to replace the amount we need quickly. Additionally, active women absorb less iron than their sedentary counterparts. We also lose iron in our sweat and have a breakdown of red blood cells in the process of tearing down and building up muscle. As a result of these factors, active women should make sure they are getting enough iron. You may want to look at iron supplements or once-a-day vitamins. Another alternative is to simply eat more red meat or other foods that are high in iron, such as pork chops, spinach, and dried apricots. One of the telltale signs that you are low in iron is feeling tired all the time or feeling lightheaded. Whether you are suffering from these symptoms or not, you might want to have your doctor check your levels with a blood test.

Foods High in Iron

The recommended daily allowance (RDA) for iron is 15 milligrams each day. Select foods from this list to ensure that you are getting the required amount of iron in your diet.

FOOD	SERVING SIZE	MG OF IRON
Cereal, ready to eat, fortified	1 cup	1–16
Clams, canned	1/4 cup	11.2
Tofu	3 oz	8.0
Beef liver, fried	3 oz	5.3
Molasses, blackstrap	1 tablespoon	5.0
Baked beans	1 cup	5.0
Oysters, cooked	1 oz	3.8
Tuna	3 oz	3.0
Baked potato, with skin	1 medium	2.8
Burrito, bean	1 medium	2.5
Beef noodle soup	1 cup	2.4
White rice, enriched	1 cup	2.3
Spinach, frozen	1/2 cup	1.5
Ground beef, lean	3 oz	1.8
Apricots, dried halves	10	1.7
Bread, whole wheat	1 slice	1.2
Broccoli, fresh cooked	1/2 cup	0.7
Egg	1	0.7

AMENORRHEA

Amenorrhea is when you no longer have your period due to insufficient levels of fat or other nutrients in the body. If you lose too much weight, you will lose your period. While some elite female athletes don't mind losing their period in the name of competition, it is not a healthy state for anyone. When your body no longer functions as it should because it is being deprived of necessary nutrients, that's a problem. Also, when your fat levels get too low, so do your levels of estrogen. This can impact your ability to have children and may make you more susceptible to osteoporosis, heart disease, and stress fractures.

FUELING UP FOR THE RUN

The most important nutrient you should be taking in before a run is water. Water, water, water. It will help keep you cool, keep your blood flowing well, and make your run more pleasurable. You should drink 8 to 12 glasses of water every day, but you should be taking in even more on the days you run. Drink 2 cups of water two hours before you run and 1 to 2 cups in the hour leading up to your run.

As for what food to take in before the run, you should be eating something high in carbohydrates about an hour or two before you run. Bananas, bagels, and crackers are examples of a few good pre-run snacks. You don't want to eat too soon before the run because it can cause stomach cramps. Alternately, if you leave too much time between eating and running, you could end up with a different kind of stomach cramp brought on my hunger. Figure out what is a good snack, and a good time to eat it, for you.

Foods high in protein are generally not suggested for pre-run snacks; some people find that they don't digest well before a run. Also, carbohydrates, not protein, are the nutrient you want to take in to fuel a workout. Another issue is osmolality, or the thickness or concentration of what you are eating or drinking. The higher the osmolality, or thickness, the more fluid your stomach needs to draw from the rest of the body to digest it. To avoid stomach cramps or dehydration (caused by your stomach and the rest of your body both being shortchanged on the hydration front), try to stay away from foods with high osmolality, such as orange juice.

EATING ON THE RUN—LITERALLY

Water

Unless it is a very hot day, you won't usually need to take water along with you on your runs if you are out there for 30 minutes or less. Beyond that, however, it becomes important to rehydrate on the go. You want to be taking in 1/3 to 2 cups of water (on hot days) for every 15 to 20 minutes you are out there. That may sound like an awful lot, but your body, and your running performance, relies on it.

Power Foods

Taking some sort of food along with you on your runs is not necessary unless you will be running for more than an hour and a half. In the first 10 to 15 minutes of running, the body uses blood glucose and glycogen to fuel exercise. Then, after 15 minutes, we use some fat too. For those interested in running's fat-burning effects, this is an important fact. Then, after about an hour and a half of running, our glycogen stores get depleted. As a result, we will start to break down muscles to continue to fuel our workout and will feel lightheaded and wobbly legged. We don't want this to happen. This is where foods like Power Gels, Power Bars, and Gatorade come in. These foods and drinks are very high in carbohydrates, and calories, and can therefore replenish our glycogen stores so that we can go on exercising. We should take in 30 to 60 grams of carbohydrates per hour during long runs. I usually don't take any power food or drink with me unless I will be running longer than 90 minutes since my body will just be running out of fuel when I get to the end of my run. If I want to go up toward two hours, however, it's critical that I bring something along with me.

One mistake I see a lot of people making is to eat and drink these products before and after runs when they haven't really gone far enough to warrant them. They are almost pure sugar, after all. They are made to fuel a person during an activity that is ongoing and must be sustained.

Another great benefit of these sport foods is that they replace electrolyte minerals like sodium and potassium. When these minerals are lost in large quantities through sweat, we can start to feel sick and lightheaded. Getting electrolytes back into a proper range is very important.

AFTER THE RUN

During the time period from about 20 minutes to about an hour after your run, you have a window of heightened opportunity to replace your glycogen stores. According to Nancy Clark, the enzymes responsible for making glycogen are most active within this time frame. For those concerned about keeping fuel stores high, it's important to eat foods that are high in carbohydrates during this period of time. You will also want some protein in your post-run meal, as protein is critical to the repair of your muscles. For your carbohydrate intake after the run, you should take in 1 gram of carbohydrate per kilogram of body weight.

Other Nutrition Tips

✔ Make healthy trade-offs.
✔ Don't be fooled by low-fat foods.
✔ Buy fresh, not packaged, foods.
✔ Take time to shop wisely.
✔ Read labels on food packages.
✔ Eat snacks during the day.
✔ Cut down on foods, don't cut them out.
✔ Fill a small plate.
✔ Pay attention to serving size.
✔ Allow fat and protein.
✔ Flavor foods in a low-fat way.
✔ Eat your food slowly.
✔ Start your day with a good breakfast.
✔ Make more than one meal at a time.
✔ Think before ordering restaurant food.

CREATE A FOOD PHILOSOPHY

You may be able to lose weight on various fad diets, but many aren't healthy, and most are not sustainable. My philosophy on weight loss and healthy eating is to never do anything that I can't promise myself I can do for a lifetime. I don't want to see how thin I can get my thighs if I run 15K every day and never eat bread. I'd probably like it, but it's not something I can maintain. I would be thrown into a never-ending cycle of weight ups and downs, probably to be followed by an eating disorder of some kind. I also don't forbid myself from eating certain foods. My husband eats pizza like it's going out of style, and I couldn't bear not to partake at least once a week. And I could not live without occasionally eating my barbecue-flavored Fritos. As I mentioned previously, after every marathon I have friends meet me with the large-sized bag of these. It's my gift to my body. I deserve it. But I can't eat these things all the time. It's all about moderation, wholesomeness, and balance. It's about what you do more often than not. It's about finding what works best for you.

CHAPTER TWELVE

INJURIES

Once you've tasted a bit of the runner's high, it's easy to become dependent on that escape down to the park. It's a great feeling, so keep it going. One of the biggest mistakes beginner runners make is to do too much, too soon, too quickly. This is especially true once the mental and physical benefits of running start showing themselves. While it's natural to want to keep those benefits coming by running more, nine times out of ten taking things too quickly results in injuries. Most casual athletes may have no trouble taking a few weeks off to heal up, but for those of us who depend on our runs for our mental health, time off can, at times, be devastating.

As I write this, my iliotibial band is enflamed, my tibialis posterior is throbbing, and my ankle still hasn't healed from being sprained twice within three weeks last month. I have decided to take a week off—and I can't tell you how hard it was for me to make that decision. I believe running has actually become a physical addiction for me. I believe I need the brain chemicals generated during my runs and I get irritable, sad, and depressed when I go for long periods of time without them; it's a kind of withdrawal. Whether or not you've developed this addiction yourself, many runners develop a more basic dependence on runs to bring things back into perspective, keep calm, or even just keep feeling physically healthy. So whatever your reason for running, it's important to keep yourself injury-free. You can't run with a serious injury, and that's pain you may feel deeper than you may have thought. By learning some preventive measures, however—knowing what can go wrong and what to do when it does—you can avoid sustaining an injury that will make you hang up your sneakers and miss those precious runs for long.

STRETCHING

While there doesn't seem to be any evidence that stretching can help to prevent injuries, it does play an important role in keeping your body healthy overall. By consistently, and properly, stretching your muscles and tendons after exercise, you realign the tissue damaged during your runs and break up scar tissue, keeping your body in the best possible state for healing. Also, stretching keeps you limber and your muscles supple, making them less likely to tear with sudden moves and more resilient to overuse damage. Stretching also helps flush the lactic acid (a by-product of exercise) out of your muscles, allowing more effective healing while helping decrease the pain after those longer or more strenuous runs. By stretching you also help with blood circulation, allowing your body to achieve overall fitness.

RUNNING SURFACES

A fundamental facet of avoiding injuries is taking a critical look at the surface you are running on. My first foray into running in public was at the indoor track at my university. The track was cambered, or slanted, at a severe angle at all four curves, so the staff there had designed a system in which runners would go in one direction one day and the other the next. As a novice runner, I didn't really understand the significance of this. But when I started to develop severe pain in my left foot, I realized it was because I went to the track every other day, meaning I ran in the same direction every time. This put an enormous amount of stress on one side of my body: One side was always contracted going around the bends while the other side was always extended.

Tracks aren't the only places where cambered running surfaces can be found. Most streets are cambered on either side to allow rainfall to drain away. If you are running on a cambered surface, make sure to spend as much time running with one side of your body contracted as you do the other side. This can be accomplished by running out to a location, then back on the same side of the road.

Be particularly careful when running on snow, ice, sand, and other uneven surfaces. Stepping on a rock is a fast way to turn over your ankle.

PROPER SHOES

Making sure you are in the proper shoes is another critical element in keeping your body healthy. If you are in cushioning shoes when you overpronate, you could end up with a number of serious problems and painful injuries. It's important to buy your running shoes from a professional who knows about running and has assessed your foot plant and gait. For more on shoe selection, see chapter 9.

BIOMECHANICS

Biomechanics, or the science of movement as it applies to the human body, is another important aspect of keeping healthy and strong throughout your running career. While there are a number of fine points to consider in your running biomechanics, those assessments are best made by a professional who has analyzed your gait and worked with you one on one. Still, here are some biomechanic basics that you can use as a guide:

- ✔ Try not to let your feet cross your midline; having your feet land just inside your hips is optimal.
- ✔ You should land on your heel first, then roll up onto your toes as you push off.
- ✔ Keep your body standing tall.
- ✔ Keep your head up and straight.

- ✔ Try not to slouch or lean to either side. (The idea is to keep your body as symmetrical as you can.)
- ✔ Your arms should be held comfortably at your sides, with hands relaxed. (Unless you are sprinting, you shouldn't be "pumping" your arms. This wastes energy. Also, keep your arms moving forward and back. Side-to-side motions take away from the forward momentum you are trying to establish.)
- ✔ Try to keep your hips forward with your buttocks comfortably tucked in and your stomach slightly contracted.

While doing all of this try to relax, if you can!

ANTI-INFLAMMATORIES

Despite the prevalence of over-the-counter anti-inflammatory medications, using these pills as treatment for athletic injuries has actually become controversial. Sections of the medical community point out the potential hazards of overuse (like bleeding of the stomach lining), yet doctors routinely prescribe anti-inflammatory ibuprofen-based drugs for many running injuries. Anti-inflammatories were the reason I was able to run my first marathon despite suffering from Achilles tendonitis. However, there is a tendency to use these drugs as a crutch to keep running. You should always follow the instructions on the package and consult your doctor if you find yourself using the medicines longer than the package suggests. Remember: Anti-inflammatories are meant to aid with healing by reducing swelling. They should not be used to mask your pain. In fact, experts say you shouldn't take them before you run because you may end up running when pain would otherwise tell you its time to stop.

R.I.C.E.

What you do in the first minutes, hours, and days after sustaining an injury or noticing an overuse injury can make a big difference in how well and how fast it heals. It's important to follow the R.I.C.E. approach to injury treatment in those critical early stages. R.I.C.E. stands for rest, ice, compression, and elevation. These are the four cornerstones to the first line of treatment for injuries. You should rest the area; ice it if it's red, warm, swollen, or painful; compress it with some sort of tensor bandage; and elevate it above your heart level as often as possible. These methods combined give the damaged area the best chance at recovery by keeping swelling down and allowing your body to heal.

PROFESSIONAL HELP

It's sometimes hard to know when to go for professional help. There are a lot of professionals available to runners to help with injuries. From your family doctor, to sports injury physicians, to athletic therapists and physiotherapists, there are many options. If the usual R.I.C.E. methods do not provide significant relief within a couple of weeks or you are unable to run at all, you should see a professional. I suggest a sports injury doctor over a general practitioner, however, since regular medical doctors usually have their sights on getting you better but not necessarily helping you keep running while you're at it. One sports injury specialist I know said she separates those "weekend warriors" or people who aren't totally committed to their sport from those who are by telling them to take two weeks off to heal. Weekend warriors usually say, "No problem," while a more committed runner would shriek at the idea and would want to know how to keep running while she heals. In any case, only you can decide when it's time to turn the case over to a professional. Additionally, only you can decide what course of treatment is best for you.

THE MOST COMMON RUNNING INJURIES

Runner's Knee (Patellar Femoral Syndrome)

Patellar femoral syndrome, or runner's knee, is the most common injury among runners, particularly women because of the increased angle from the hip to knee. The injury occurs as a result of the kneecap moving out of its usual up-and-down groove at the end of the femur (upper leg bone). When the kneecap moves side to side, it rubs against the femur, causing the pain known as runner's knee. It is a classic overuse injury. This injury can actually develop into chondromalacia or the wearing away of the cartilage under the kneecap, a condition that can't be reversed.

SYMPTOMS

✔ Pain around kneecap
✔ Stiffness in knee
✔ Swelling

TREATMENT

✔ R.I.C.E.
✔ New shoes for ankle pronation
✔ Anti-inflammatories
✔ Stretching hamstrings and quadriceps
✔ Strengthening exercises for hamstrings and quads
✔ Rubber sleeve to hold kneecap in place
✔ Orthotics
✔ Surgery

CAUSES

✔ Overpronation
✔ High mileage
✔ Weak quadriceps
✔ Strength imbalance between hamstrings and quadriceps
✔ Misalignment of kneecap

Achilles Tendonitis

The Achilles tendon connects the two large muscles in the calf to the back of your heelbone. Running causes these muscles to tighten up, which can lead to inflammation or tearing of the Achilles tendon. This is known as Achilles tendonitis.

SYMPTOMS

✔ Pinpointed soreness on back of heel
✔ Stabbing, dull, or sharp pain

✔ Redness in area
✔ Warmth in area
✔ Area feels better farther into a run

TREATMENT
✔ R.I.C.E.
✔ Calf stretches
✔ Heel lift
✔ Anti-inflammatory medication
✔ Tendon stretches, followed by icing
✔ Wearing street shoes with heels to relieve the tension
✔ Casting
✔ Surgery
✔ Physiotherapy

CAUSES
✔ Tight calves
✔ Overpronation
✔ Insufficient warm-up
✔ Sudden sprints
✔ Shoes rubbing back of heel

Tibial Stress Syndrome

Tibial stress syndrome is sometimes incorrectly referred to as shin-splints. It is a condition caused by minute tears in the shin muscles where they attach to the bone. They can occur on the front (anterior) of the shin, on the posterior side (back of tibia), or along the fibula or small lower leg bone.

SYMPTOMS
✔ Pain along shin or fibula

TREATMENT
✔ Ice
✔ Stretching
✔ Reduced mileage
✔ Strengthening exercises

CAUSES

✔ Tightness in muscles in lower leg
✔ Overpronation
✔ Weakness in tibialis anterior (front shin)
✔ Shock

Hamstring Pull

A hamstring pull is an inflammation or tearing of the muscle at the back of your thigh. This injury most often occurs during sudden movements, as in sprinting or speed training. However, it can also happen over time from overuse.

SYMPTOMS

✔ Sharp, localized pain in back of thigh
✔ Black-and-blue discoloration
✔ Dull ache
✔ Tight sensation

TREATMENT

✔ R.I.C.E.
✔ Anti-inflammatory medication
✔ Gentle stretching

Ankle Sprains

Virtually everyone has experienced an ankle sprain at one time or another, but runners are particularly susceptible to this very painful and potentially troublesome injury. An ankle sprain occurs when the foot accidentally rolls over, causing an unnatural positioning of the foot, straining or spraining the muscles on the top of the foot. One sprain can leave the foot weak and susceptible to sprains in the future.

SYMPTOMS

✔ Pain on top of foot
✔ Swelling
✔ Coloring of injured area

TREATMENT

✔ R.I.C.E.
✔ Foot- and ankle-strengthening exercises
✔ Physiotherapy
✔ Brace
✔ Casting
✔ Surgery
✔ Avoiding unstable surfaces

CAUSES

✔ Stepping on uneven, unstable surface
✔ Tripping

Iliotibial Band Friction Syndrome

Iliotibial band friction syndrome is one of the most feared injuries among runners. The iliotibial band is composed of fasciae that run from the hip down the outside of the thigh along the outside of the knee before connecting to the tibia just below the knee. Pain is felt at the outside of the knee when the band becomes inflamed from rubbing on the side of the knee.

SYMPTOMS

✔ Dull, sharp pain on outside of knee
✔ Pain leaves when not running
✔ Pain in hip where band crosses bursa sac

TREATMENT

✔ R.I.C.E.
✔ Change shoes
✔ Change running surface
✔ Cushioned insoles
✔ Flexibility exercises: stretch hamstrings, quads, and ITB
✔ Anti-inflammatory medication
✔ Strength exercises
✔ Orthotics
✔ Physiotherapy

CAUSES

- ✔ Overpronation
- ✔ Underpronation
- ✔ Incorrect shoes
- ✔ High mileage and increased intensity of runs
- ✔ Running on cambered surface
- ✔ Inflexibility/no stretching
- ✔ Poor gait; crossing over of feet
- ✔ Downhill training
- ✔ Leg-length disparity

Plantar Fasciitis

Plantar fasciitis is a condition affecting the long fibrous band of tissue at the bottom of your foot running from your toes, traveling up the arch of your foot, and inserting in your heel.

SYMPTOMS

- ✔ Pain like a bruise under your heel
- ✔ Pain in heel that is worst in the morning and diminishes during day
- ✔ Pulling or tearing sensation in arch or heel

TREATMENT

- ✔ Ice
- ✔ Rest
- ✔ Massage
- ✔ Taping
- ✔ Heel pads
- ✔ Anti-inflammatory medication
- ✔ Orthotics or heel lifts
- ✔ Flexibility exercises (calf stretches)
- ✔ Strength exercises

CAUSES

- ✔ Excessive pronation
- ✔ High arches
- ✔ Incorrect sport or daily-use shoes
- ✔ Overuse

Shinsplints

The term *shinsplints* actually refers to a number of different minor injuries that can cause a dull pain in the front of the lower leg. Most frequently this pain is caused by either inflammation of the muscles on the shin or inflammation of the thin sheath of tissue that surrounds the shinbone.

SYMPTOMS

- ✔ Throbbing pain along inside or outside of shin
- ✔ Tenderness when touched

TREATMENT

- ✔ R.I.C.E.
- ✔ Anti-inflammatories
- ✔ Stretching calves
- ✔ Checking proper shoes
- ✔ Rest
- ✔ Slow pace

CAUSES

ANTERIOR SHINSPLINTS

- ✔ High arches
- ✔ Supination
- ✔ Tight calves
- ✔ Loose shoes
- ✔ Shock

POSTERIOR SHINSPLINTS

- ✔ Collapsed arches
- ✔ Pronation
- ✔ Training on hard surfaces
- ✔ Shock

Stress Fractures

Stress fractures are very small, incomplete breaks or cracks in the bone that form as a result of repeated stress or pounding. They are most commonly found on your shins or metatarsals of your feet (the bones behind the toes) and less frequently in the pelvis and hip areas. Unfortunately, these stress fractures don't show up in X rays until they are well on their way to healing.

SYMPTOMS

✔ Acute, sharp pain in pinpointed area

✔ Muscle soreness in the injured area

TREATMENT

✔ R.I.C.E.

✔ Anti-inflammatories

✔ Stopping running

CAUSE

✔ Stress of pounding when running

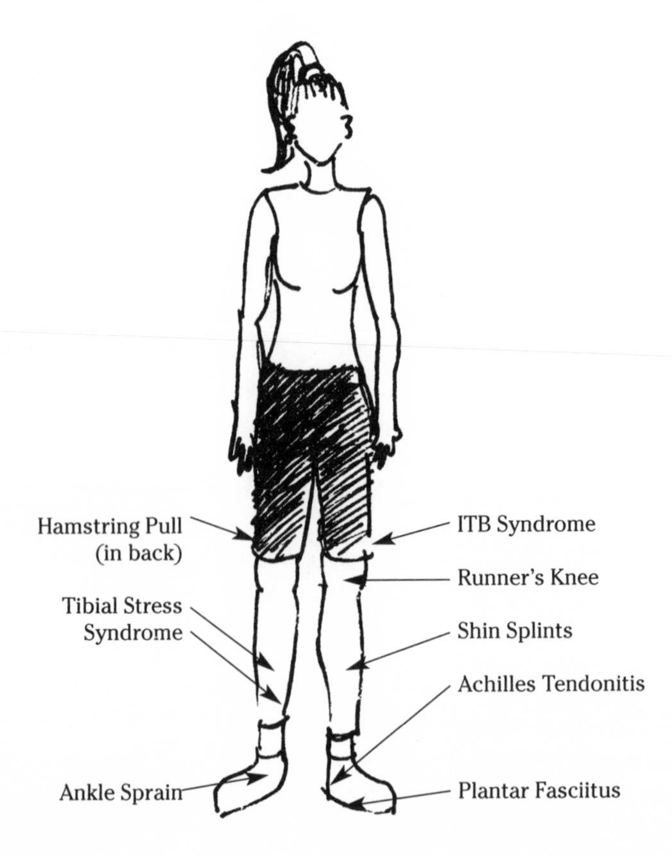

WHEN YOU'RE SICK

Another time when you may want to rethink heading out for a run is when you are ill. The rule of thumb is that you shouldn't run if you have any symptoms from the neck down or have a fever. If it's just a head cold without a fever, you can probably work out safely, although your performance may not be the best. In fact, running can actually help clear your head and make you feel a little better when you have a cold. But if that illness is also coupled with a hacking cough that has things rumbling around in your lungs, you might want to think about taking some time off. It may be a sign that you're developing, or have, a chest infection of some kind, and running could make it worse. And if you have the stomach flu or a fever, you really shouldn't be running. Running will heat your body up—something that you don't want to do when your body temperature is already elevated to an uncomfortable level. However, if you're just feeling a little queasy in your stomach, sometimes going for a run can help alleviate that. It's up to you to decide if you are up to a run when you are ill. But remember, your body is already working overtime to get you better, so if you do run, don't expect too much of yourself and take it easy.

FILLING IN THE GAPS

While running can significantly strengthen certain muscles in our body, particularly in our legs, the sport can leave some smaller muscles comparatively underdeveloped, according to marathon runner and sports injury therapist Cheryl Nix of Toronto's Competitive Edge Performance Therapy. "Sometimes these weak points can lead to injuries," she says. "So doing strengthening exercises is a good way to both heal and prevent injuries." Left unchallenged, underdeveloped muscles can lead to a variety of injuries.

Before we take a look at some simple, yet effective exercises to beef up those weaker muscles, we need to go over a couple of pieces of equipment you'll need:

✔ **ANKLE WEIGHTS:** These are sand-filled bags, usually found in 2- or 5-pound varieties, that can be easily Velcroed around your ankles or wrists. They should be strapped on tight enough so that they don't move, but not so tight that they cut off the blood flow. These weights can be found in specialty sports stores or in the sports departments of most department stores. For the purposes of these exercises, the 2-pound weights are preferred.

✔ **THERABAND:** This is a simple strip of a light rubber material that can be cut to any length and used like a long rubber band. Tying each end in a loop allows you to wrap one end around a foot or an ankle while holding the other end. These may be a little harder to find than the ankle weights. Physical therapists of all kinds often hand them out for free to their clients; or you can find them through many physiotherapy supply distributors.

Buttocks (Gluteus Maximus)

Surprisingly, our butts are not given a really good workout with most moderately paced distance running, according to Nix. "They usually don't get worked too hard unless you are doing speedwork or a lot of hills," she notes. "Women in particular tend to have a shorter stride, so sometimes they don't even really use it." The gluteus maximus is a push-off muscle that works in conjunction with our calf and quadriceps muscles when we push off the ground with our toes. Weakness in this muscle can lead to hip joint problems, overuse injuries of the hamstrings, and sacroiliac problems.

Try the following exercise to strengthen your buttocks: Wearing ankle weights or using a Theraband, stand up tall, balance on one leg, bend your other knee, and pull it up and back. Do 15 to 25 repeats with both legs.

Outside Hip Muscles (Gluteus Medius and Gluteus Minimus)

These muscles are critical to stabilizing our pelvis when we run. As we come up off the ground in midstride, these muscles are used (or should be) to hold our pelvis in a level position. They are particularly critical for women since we have wider hips and therefore a greater angle from our hips to our knees, Nix says. Weakness in these muscles can lead to the very painful iliotibial band friction syndrome (because the ITB is being forced to help stabilize the hips), knee-tracking problems, and various hip, pelvis, and lower back problems.

Try the following exercises to strengthen these muscles: Using a Theraband or ankle weights, balance on one leg by using your hip muscles to stabilize your body (it's actually your balancing leg that is being targeted by this exercise). Then raise your other leg out to your side and lower it again. Do 15 to 25 repeats on both legs.

Smaller, Inside Quadriceps Muscle (Vastus Medialis)

This muscle is critical to maintaining the proper tracking of the kneecap. Most runners tend to have a stronger vastus lateralis, or outside quadriceps muscle, causing an imbalance between the two. Weakness here can lead to various kneecap-tracking-related problems and tendonitis.

Try the following exercise to beef up your vastus medialis: With your feet parallel and about shoulder distance apart, hold your arms out in front of your body and lower yourself down into a squatting position. Go down as far as you can comfortably, then come up. Do 15 to 20 repeats.

Front Shin Muscle

(Tibialis Anterior)

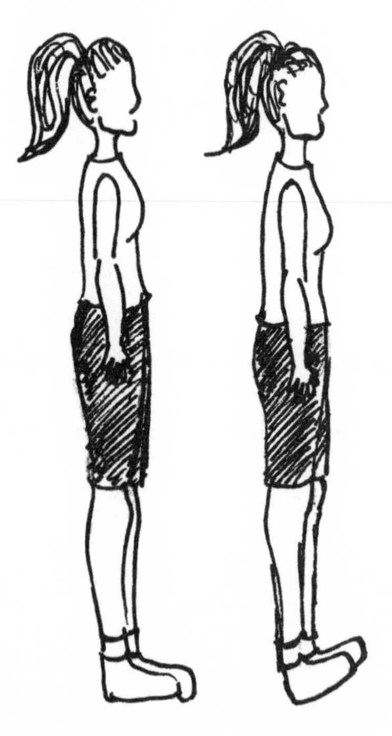

This muscle is critical to the toe-lifting portion of our running gait. Women who wear high-heeled shoes often have particularly weak shin muscles because these muscles are left in the stretched position for long periods of time. Weakness in these muscles can lead to shinsplints, stress fractures, and tendonitis.

The following exercise can help you strengthen these muscles: Standing with your feet comfortably apart, raise your toes up off the ground so that you are balancing on your heels, then relax your toes back to the ground. Repeat 25 to 30 times.

Deep Calf Muscle (Tibialis Posterior)

This muscle is a major supporter of our arch, and with so many of us overpronating to some degree, this can be a common spot of weakness. As your foot rolls in, this muscle is placed in the elongated position, making it weaker. Weakness in this muscle can lead to plantar fasciitis, tendonitis, patellar femoral syndrome, and other knee-joint problems.

Try the following exercise to strengthen the tibialis posterior: Stand on one foot with your foot relaxed. Lift your arch up, go up onto your toes, then lower your heel back to the ground (without relaxing your arch back down to floor). Holding your arch up, go back up onto your toes and repeat 15 to 20 times on each foot.

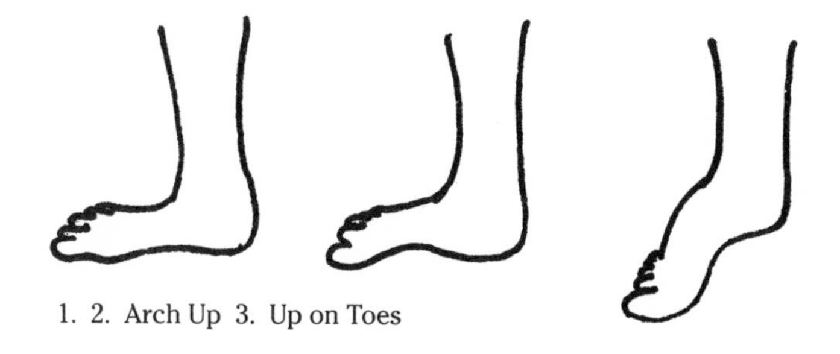

1. 2. Arch Up 3. Up on Toes

CHERYL'S TOP 10 MISTAKES RUNNERS MAKE

1. Doing too much, too soon.
2. Ignoring body strain and pain.
3. Running on a track in the same direction.
4. Running on the slope of the road.
5. Lack of stretching.
6. Wearing worn-out or improper shoes.
7. Failing to alternate easy run days with harder days.
8. Running on excessively hard surfaces.
9. Not cross-training.
10. Not seeking professional help.

KEEPING HEALTHY

I remember sitting in an outdoor café with my husband, choking back tears because I had broken my toe and was forced to take time off in the middle of training for my third marathon. I was depressed by the fact that I had put so much time and energy into something, and it might have been all for nothing. I wanted another marathon under my belt; I knew I could do better than I had in my last race. But what was upsetting me the most was that I couldn't run at all. I need my runs. My mental health depends on it. By sustaining a number of injuries over my years of running, which caused both physical and emotional pain, I have learned the hard way how important it is to take precautions and know what to do when an injury strikes you. By following the advice in this chapter, you should be able to avoid any prolonged absences from your precious escapes to the park.

CHAPTER THIRTEEN

Safety on the Run

That blissful, incoherent daze I wrote about in chapter 7 is great for your emotional state of mind, but it can make running a dangerous sport for women. While zoning out is the goal, we must take certain measures to ensure that we do this safely. That means making good decisions and always keeping your wits about you. It may sound like a contradiction, but it is possible to zone out and stay alert. While running itself causes most injuries, the most serious injuries can be sustained as a result of factors outside our control.

RUNNERS AS PREY

The female jogger has practically become the cliché rape victim. Whether it's based on statistics or just common use in fiction, people often think of the risk of rape when they think of a woman running alone. There have been a number of high-profile rape cases involving female runners over the years and in countries around the world, but that doesn't mean as runners we are any more likely to be assaulted than the average woman. The nature of running, however, does present increased opportunities for rapists, muggers, and other predators to attack. We often run alone, we prefer more scenic, therefore more isolated, surroundings, and we can attract attention with the clothing we wear. None of this, however, should dissuade us from running. We wouldn't want to go back to a time when women were discouraged from exploring the world. But what we must do is take precautions to ensure we don't get hurt.

Criminals aren't the only considerations for runners, however. Cars, cyclists, harassers, and animals are just a few other obstacles that can stand in the way of a safe, fun run. In each case, using common sense is the best course of action.

RUNNING AT NIGHT

A good rule of thumb is to avoid running at night if at all possible. Fewer people are on the streets at night, it's harder to see what's going on after dark, and it seems more undesirables come out after dark. However, it's not always possible, with our busy lives, to get our runs in during daylight, especially during the shorter days of fall and winter. If you are going to run at night, then, it is wise to run in well-populated areas. Unfortunately, this often means running on the sidewalks through not-so-scenic areas, but your safety is worth the sacrifice. Running through parks or other wooded areas after dark alone is not something I encourage. If you must, however, do it with a group of people, or at least a partner. There is indeed safety in numbers.

Safety devices like pepper spray, buzzers, and whistles can be helpful additions to your protection plan, but don't rely on them. In the panic of the moment, you may not even think to use them; they might not have the desired effect; and if you wield a weapon, it could be used on you. It's critical that you take other precautions, like running where it's safer. Taking a self-defense course is another great idea. While instructors of these courses admit you'll probably forget most of what you learn in the class, you will likely leave with one or two great moves that could mean the difference between getting away from an attacker and being assaulted.

Never wear a portable radio headset. If you need tunes to keep you running and help you zone out, don't run at night. If you can't hear what's going on around you, an attacker can sneak up behind you without you even knowing. It's critical that you keep your senses alert when you run. It's also important to vary your running routes. Many rapists plan out their attacks well in advance, and seeing a woman run the same route on the same days at the same times makes this job a lot easier. Keep them guessing. Don't be predictable.

One of the reasons I started to run was the thought that if a man wanted to attack me, I'd have no chance whatsoever of outrunning him in my overweight, unhealthy condition. As I progressed in my running, however, I realized I'd have no chance of outrunning a man, period. Even though I have run marathons and other races in times most men never could, in a short sprint, men can beat most women hands-down. They have bigger muscles, larger hearts, and more lung capacity, and with testosterone pumping, most women would never have a chance in a short chase. So don't assume your newfound running ability will in itself protect you.

DOGS AND OTHER WILDLIFE

Dogs and runners often do not mix. Dogs like to chase anyone or anything that's running. On a couple of occasions I've had dogs chase me and jump up to nip my arms. Fortunately, I've never been hurt, but other runners haven't been as lucky. Running with a veteran runner during a marathon training run one morning, we passed a dog that proceeded to jump up onto us. The dog's owner yelled, "Don't worry, he doesn't bite," and my run partner replied, "I've been bitten by three dogs that don't bite." I think the best approach is to stop running and walk past any dogs that seem to be taking an interest in you. Make it clear to the dog's owner that you've been inconvenienced by the dog, and start running again only when he's gotten control of the animal. I love dogs, but many dogs don't like strange runners passing by, so I treat every one I run past with caution.

With all of that said, your own dog can be an excellent run partner and help protect you from predators and other dangers during your run. It's also a great way for your furry friend to get some exercise and for you to fit walking the dog into your busy schedule. You should check with breeders and other animal specialists before getting a dog to run with, however, as many breeds are prone to hip problems or don't make good running dogs for other reasons.

While it is rare, there have been a number of reported bear maulings involving folks going for a run through the woods across North America. Because of the speed we're moving at, runners can come upon a bear quickly, causing the animal to panic. Most often bears hear us coming and will move away before we arrive, but runners can sometimes surprise them. No one can outrun a bear, so if you want to run through the woods, you'd be wise to stick to well-worn paths and areas where people often go. Bears tend to steer clear of these areas. Don't forget: Bear attacks are often fatal.

If you are going to go for runs in the woods, snakes and birds are other animals you might want to look out for. There have been reports of birds diving out of the sky and "attacking" runners. And while snakes most often will not attack, if they are stepped on (something runners could inadvertently do moving quickly through the woods), they will bite. Again, keep your wits about you. And remember that poison ivy, poison oak, and poison sumac will make your life miserable if your skin touches their leaves. Get to know the area you are running in, and cover any exposed skin that may come in contact with poisonous plants or sharp flora.

CARS AND OTHER OBSTACLES

Cars truly are a runner's enemy. A collision between a runner and a car may turn out in the runner's favor in a civil courtroom, but nowhere else. Cars are the ones with the coat of armor, so it's critical that you make eye contact with the drivers of any cars coming near your path. This is particularly important at corners, where drivers are getting ready to make a turn and are focused primarily on other cars. Stop at the corner and be sure the driver has seen you before proceeding into the intersection. Never assume. We've all seen drivers proceed to make a turn, then suddenly stop when they realize a pedestrian is in their path. It's as though they never bothered to consider traffic other than vehicles. Proceed as though every driver is out to hit you.

Wearing reflective gear or strips of reflective material on your running clothes is essential if you are running after dark. Drivers literally cannot see you otherwise. But with those reflective strips, your body lights up the second their headlights hit you. If they can't see you, they can't avoid you.

While concrete is about 10 percent harder than asphalt, running on the road is a risky business. If you are going to run on the road, run facing the oncoming traffic. That way, if the driver doesn't see you, you will at least have a chance to jump out of the way. If the cars are coming from behind you, you won't have a chance. Also, be aware of the sun. Drivers are often blinded by sunlight; it's been the cause of many fatalities. In fact, traffic cops say more accidents happen on sunny days than on slick rainy days. So if the sun is low in the sky, you'd be smart to move to the sidewalks or trails.

USE THE BUDDY SYSTEM

Group running is by far the safest way to run. Few attackers would dare make a move on five people thundering down a city street. Run partners can also help you avoid other dangers, like a car you didn't see or a branch you are about to trip over. If you are running behind others, however, make sure they call out any obstructions on the road; you may not see them in time to react. You can find others to run with through local running stores or run clubs or by putting up a notice at your local gym.

The buddy system also works with those who don't come out with you on your runs. When I lived with my parents, my mother would always check the clock and say, "How long will you be?" as I headed out the door. On a few occasions I saw my father driving his car along my run route when I decided to go farther than I had planned. They knew what my route was, so they'd be able to find me if I was still out there to be found. It's a good idea to get someone at home involved. If something were to happen to you, they might not be able to help right away, but they could certainly get the police involved as soon as possible if they know exactly how long you've been missing.

DON'T GET LOST

Believe it or not, I once got lost during a 10K fun run in downtown Toronto. It was a cancer benefit run that participants could take part in at any time during the day. I made the mistake of not paying attention to the map, then following another runner who turned out to be on his own personal run that day. Needless to say, I ended up nowhere close to where I should have been. Fortunately, Toronto has the CN Tower, the tallest freestanding structure in the world, and I knew it was south, so I just found the tower on the skyline and ran. I soon figured out where I was, but it sure was upsetting to be lost. This is even more true if you are running in the woods or someplace you don't know well. Make sure you know exactly where you are going to ensure a fun run.

Other Tips

✔ Bring ID in case anything should happen to you.
✔ Carry change for a phone call or cash for a cab home.
✔ Don't wear jewelry that will catch a robber's eye.
✔ Avoid running past parked cars and bushes.
✔ Be careful approaching just-parked cars.
✔ Ignore verbal harassment.
✔ Trust your gut instincts.

WHEN SOMETHING DOES GO WRONG

I once had a man grab my crotch while I was running; another man followed me through a park. In both cases I called the police, but the men were never found. Sometimes women are afraid to call the police or feel that what happened wasn't serious enough to report. But you should ask yourself, "Do I want this guy out here when I go for my next run?" Don't forget that predators' actions tend to escalate with each incident. If all he did was grab a body part one day, that doesn't mean he won't be pulling someone into a bush the next. He may also be wanted in another crime. It's important that you report any suspicious situations, too, and trust your "spider senses." A veteran cop once told me that if your gut tells you something is not right, it probably isn't.

While it's easy enough to say "remain calm" during an attack, when you are in the middle of it, that truly is a hard thing to do. I've been the victim of a few crimes and each time I feel like I'm in a Peanuts television special. You know how all the adults' voices sound like "wa-wa, wa-wa-wa, wa"? Well, that's the way everyone sounds to me during an attack. I think it's a side effect of shock, but you really are in a vulnerable position because you've been caught off guard. However, if you concentrate on breathing, you should be able to pull yourself together enough to act. What you do during the incident depends on what's happening and your own personal views on what you should do. In some cases, fighting hard and running is your best bet. In others, it may be advisable to just do whatever the perpetrator tells you to do. In any case, try to breathe and make sound decisions.

Eye Contact

Women's running heroine Katherine Switzer offers some excellent advice in her book *Running and Walking for Women Over 40: The Road to Sanity and Vanity*. She says your body language can be a powerful defense against attacks. "When lost in thought and feeling free, what we often signal to predators is that we're someone who is vulnerable and easily surprised," she writes. Switzer suggests keeping aware of your body language and facial expressions, presenting a powerful, if relaxed, impression. Making brief eye contact with people you pass by is another way of telling people that you are not afraid of them and also lets potential attackers know that you've seen their face.

With all of these dangers to consider, you might be thinking of heading for your local indoor track right about now. While that is a safer option (if the track is well populated), relying on a track for your runs can make fitting run time into your life harder. I for one also find tracks extremely boring to run on. They tend to be smelly, too! If you are like me and prefer the open air, just make sure you've taken the right precautions and are prepared.

PART III

STICKING WITH IT FOR LIFE

CHAPTER FOURTEEN

GET ADDICTED

Addiction is not a word that's usually used in a positive context. Most times it refers to dependence on drugs, alcohol, gambling, or other vices. But I believe there are good addictions, including the addiction to running. Many runners say that as a result of a number of physical and psychological factors, they have grown dependent on their runs. With all the enormous benefits running offers, I encourage this. Let running become your way of coping; let those daily jaunts to the park become a part of what makes you feel whole.

That said, anything can become a problem in extremes. I am not suggesting that you run two hours a day, every day, at the expense of your personal and professional life. Nor am I advocating exercise to the extreme in an obsessive plot to be as thin as you can be. I am simply saying that given how hard it is for some of us to stay motivated to keep healthy, it's a good idea to let running become a necessary part of your life.

THE POINT OF NO RETURN

I didn't realize I was addicted to running until I had to stop after a tonsillectomy when I was 21. I had been running 30K each week religiously for two years and had to stop for at least two weeks due to the risk of bleeding. While the operation itself had a depressing effect on me, I am convinced that the severely diminished mood I had following the surgery was largely attributable to the fact that I was deprived of my usual stress-relieving method and that good vibe from the brain chemicals released during my runs. I also fretted about gaining weight and had more time on my hands than usual. As they say, an idle mind is the devil's playground. All of these factors came together to make me nuts in those few weeks after the operation. But once I got back into running, I felt I had taken control again. After that, I knew that I wasn't going to be able to stop running for any significant amount of time without side effects. It was then that I knew running was going to be a part of my life forever.

IS IT TRULY ADDICTIVE?

There's been a great deal of research into the idea that running is addictive. And experts fail to agree on just what it is about running that makes it appear that runners become dependent. Some say it stimulates the release of certain hormones inside the brain, the endorphins or enkephalins, that give runners pleasurable feelings. They say the brain then becomes dependent on these pleasure-producing substances just like it can with drugs like heroine, cocaine, or morphine. Still, while no one contests the fact that running does bring on pleasurable feelings, and at the same time triggers the release of these neurotransmitters, it has not been concluded definitively that it's the endorphins that cause the peak in our mood. Evidence has shown that the degree to which the levels of endorphins rise correlates with the increase in good feelings brought on by the exercise, and that blocking the action of these endorphins does prevent some of the euphoric feelings common after running. But experts can't say whether the addictive nature of running is truly connected to endorphins.

Meanwhile, studies have shown that there can be significant withdrawal symptoms associated with stopping running. These symptoms include guilt, irritability, tension, restlessness, and depression. Other studies, however, indicate that withdrawal symptoms suffered by runners who are forced to stop running for a period of time are predominantly psychological, not physical. Whatever the truth, the bottom line is that many runners report that the side effects of stopping running are so severe and such an upset to their lives that they are afraid to stop. In one study, the researcher was unable to find daily exercisers who would participate in an experiment in which they would be paid to stop exercising for a month. In fact, many of those asked said no amount of money would change their minds. As a result, the researcher was forced to study those who exercised three times per week. The study ultimately revealed that a monthlong period without exercise impaired sleep, increased sexual tension, and increased the need to be with others.

For many runners, the cause behind the addiction is irrelevant. They know they need their runs, period. It's their drug, and considering the other options for dealing with stress, I think running is a rather healthy one.

WHEN IS IT TOO MUCH?

Now that I have sung the praises of running as an addiction, I must add there are cases of people going too far. Runners tend to be obsessive and compulsive by nature, which can lead to an unhealthy lifestyle that includes too much running. Running is actually one of the preferred sports among those with eating disorders. That's likely because of how efficient it is at burning calories. I remember running through the woods one day with my training partner and seeing a girl run past who looked like a skeleton. Her buttocks were concave. I was shocked at the speed she was running. I don't know where that energy was coming from. But I do know it wasn't going to last long. Nor, it seemed, was she. I must caution all women who read this book and hear me go on about getting addicted and how great running is to make sure they are not using their running as a part of an unhealthy lifestyle. For more on eating disorders, turn to chapter 11.

You don't have to suffer from an eating disorder to be going too far with your running, however. Some people get so obsessed with going for their runs that they neglect many more important things in their lives. Spouses, children, careers, and other vital parts of our lives can suffer if running takes up too much of our time. While this can happen within a healthy lifestyle for competitive runners, some amateur runners have been known to push it too far. If other parts of your life are suffering because of your need to run, you may have a problem. I encourage people to run to improve their lives, not replace their lives. It's unhealthy if the very aspects of your life that you started running to improve suffer because of your addiction. Let running become something you need, but keep your life in balance.

RUN FOR LIFE

I need my runs and I'm not interested in spending any time having to deal with the stresses of life without my trusty coping mechanism. I think many runners worry about a day when a doctor will tell them their knees just can't do it anymore. I cut short my last marathon training season for this very reason. My ITB was flaring up and I had a discussion with a woman who said, "Well, you know, you may have to take a few months off to heal, but after that you'll be fine." While I probably could have continued with the high mileage for the eight weeks that remained, with a compromised race finish no doubt, my fear of having to take any significant amount of time off running made me stop. Running, period, means more to me than running marathons. I want to be running well into my 70s; I need to continue to run into my 70s.

CHAPTER FIFTEEN

Racing

Racing is the best way I know of to make a lifelong commitment to running. It makes you feel like a part of the running community; it gives you a day of pride that you will never forget. Race day can be used as a celebration of how far you have come both physically and emotionally with your running. No matter what level you are at, it is possible to achieve your race distance goal if you simply follow the appropriate training programs and have a little faith. I think most runners who are new to racing are surprised by how far they really can go. My very first race was a 10K. I chose this race because I wasn't aware of all the 5K races there were available. I signed up expecting to run only half of it, but finished the entire thing with virtual ease. I was so proud of myself that I ran across the finish line in tears. After that race, I was hooked on running. There was no going back. Knowing this, I encourage anyone who is starting running, or has been doing so sporadically, to sign up for a race and come on over to "the other side."

I think many new runners are intimidated by running races. Many of my students announce that they have no intention of running the planned race at the end of the program. While I understand that some may feel it's too much for them, most are surprised by how well they do. One student of mine joined up because there was no walk club available. He insisted on being left at the back of the group to walk.

I encouraged him to try throwing in some run minutes here and there, and he eventually went along with it. Before you knew it, he was running more than he was walking. And by the end, he ran the entire 5K race. Last I checked he was the 4K-route leader at our local run club. Now he's giving new runners pep talks and encouraging them to try a race themselves. Racing not only lets you get to feel the thrill of victory, but it also helps you stay motivated and improve your running. Most importantly, however, race day can be a really good time, a great place to meet people and provide memories you will never forget.

CHOOSING A RACE

The race you choose to run depends on a number of factors, the most important of which is your running ability. If you are a beginner runner, regardless of how novice, I encourage you to try a 5K/3.1-mile race. These races are plentiful in most major cities throughout almost the entire year. For those who have been running for at least half an hour three times a week for some time, I suggest a 10K race. A 15K race is the next step, followed by the half-marathon. Your weekly mileage should be around 30K before you consider a 15K and closer to 40K before considering a half-marathon. Those looking to try a marathon should have a half-marathon under the belt and be up to about 50K per week, including one weekly long run, before starting marathon training.

I have met a number of people over the years who have tried to skip from a 5K to marathon training and soon found that injuries made it impossible for them to go on. No matter what your level of running, you shouldn't increase your weekly mileage by more than 10 percent per week in order to avoid hurting yourself. Take the time to slowly work up your way up to each race. Trying to do too much, too soon, too fast will ultimately lead to injury. Additionally, if you are unable to finish the race feeling strong, you may become disenchanted with running or discouraged from trying another race. Work up to it slowly; let each event be one you feel good about.

Local running or athletic stores usually have dozens of pamphlets and application forms for races coming up in your community. You can even log on to the Web sites of area running clubs, which often have listings of upcoming events. Running magazines also provide listings of some of the larger races across North America and the world. You may need to sign up early to ensure you get a spot behind the starting line, so check out what's coming up well in advance. Many races are also held in support of a wide array of charities, with organizers encouraging runners to collect pledges before the race. You may want to pick a race that's in support of a cause close to your heart, so look around and see what's available. As well, the Avon running series offers women-only races, allowing women to feel united with their sisters while feeling more relaxed during the race.

PREPARING TO RACE

The critical element in preparing for a race is following the right training program. These programs can range from 10 weeks for a 5K race up to 18 weeks for a marathon. You may need to slowly increase your mileage before starting one of these programs if your mileage is not already close to the range you'll be starting with in week one. Plan ahead and make sure you won't be making too big of a leap in mileage when you start your training officially. I call this pretraining training. Some say you should triple the distance of the race and make sure that your total weekly mileage exceeds that amount before running the race. However, I've had success with training less than this. For instance, I ran my first half-marathon with a weekly mileage base of just 35K, when this theory would suggest I should have been running 60K-plus weekly. Following this advice would come in handy when your finishing time is more important to you than just finishing. If this is the first time you have run a race of a particular distance, I suggest you think only about finishing; worry about improving on your time in the next race. Running the full distance of the race is another tidbit of racing advice that's often handed out. For me, and for most beginner to intermediate runners, I find this takes the punch out of the race. Again, however, this advice comes in handy for those who are working on shaving those excess minutes off their finishing time.

Following your schedule as closely and consistently as possible is critical to success on race day. Don't miss runs unless you are sick or an injury demands you take time off. Your best chance for success come race day is to have done the mileage required. There's no need to fret if you've had to miss a week due to illness or an injury, but missing a period of time longer than that will erode the fitness level you have worked to achieve. Stick to the schedule and try to keep on top of it. Eating well and getting plenty of rest is also important during this time. Think about how well Olympic athletes take care of themselves. There's no need for you to follow the strict regimens they adhere to, but thinking of yourself as an athletic competitor who wants her body in peak form can help inspire you to stay on course.

LEADING UP TO RACE DAY

Your preparation for race day should start several days before the race. Make sure that you are eating well, getting plenty of sleep, and drinking tons of water. Being properly hydrated is most important the day before and the day of the race. Carry a water bottle around with you all day on the day before the race and make sure that your urine is clear before you go to bed. You may also want to pick out your outfit for the run the day before and be sure you've got everything you'll need. If possible, pick up your race kit before race day. That way you can pin your bib onto your shirt ahead of time and avoid the worry of lining up for your package minutes before the gun goes off. Make sure you pack some warmer clothing that you can wear over your race clothes after the run, when you'll be cool. Your blood sugar plummets after a race, and being all sweaty, you'll get cool very quickly, even on warm days.

RACE DAY

There's lot to keep in mind on race day. When you first get up, start hydrating again. You'll want your urine to stay clear, but keep in mind that you'll have to make sure you've used the washroom before lining up behind the starting line. Eat what your normally eat before a run and eat it the same amount of time before your run as you usually do. Doing anything new or unusual with regard to your digestive tract can spell disaster during a race. That goes for the food you eat the night before. Do what's been tried and tested.

You'll also want to get up early enough that you'll be able to get to the race site early. You'll want to check your bag, scope out where the starting line is, and do some stretching. Most importantly, though, you'll want to check out the route and *where it ends*. It's important to know where the finish line is so that you'll know how much farther you'll have to go near the end of the race. I've run races where I thought the finish was in one place—only to turn the corner and see that I had as much as another kilometer to go! Not fun. Find out where you're running so you'll be prepared.

Check your bag at the baggage check and pick a piece of grass or sidewalk to do some stretching. You want your body to be warmed up before the race, particularly if you plan to give it your all. Many races have an organized warm-up show, with a performer on a stage leading all the runners through some light aerobic warm-up moves. This can be a great way to get blood flowing and feel like a part of the festivities.

Pick your spot behind the starting line wisely. Make sure you're not too far up, to avoid being trampled by faster runners. But also, don't position yourself too far back. You don't want to have to waste energy maneuvering around slower runners. Some races feature "pace bunnies"— people in some sort of costume who run a specific pace and whom you can line up behind. Not all pace bunnies run the correct pace, however. I once followed a pace bunny who went too quickly, forcing me to drop back and reassess my pace.

Make sure you head over to the race start early. You don't want to have to race to the start before the run even begins. Unfortunately, this has happened to me a number of times because of the lineups for the washrooms at the half- and full marathons.

RUNNING THE RACE

Once the gun goes off, check your watch or set its chronograph function so that you'll know exactly how long it takes you to run the race. There is something called your gun time and your chip time. The gun time refers to the amount of time it takes you to cross the finish line after the gun goes off, while the chip time refers to the amount of time it takes you to finish the race starting from the time you cross the starting line. That's pretty important in larger races, where it can sometimes take several minutes for you to even to get to the starting line. The microchip, which many races today have runners attach to their shoes, measures this exact time by taking a reading as your foot hits a computer pad at the start and finish lines. It's important that you step fully on the mats as you cross them. Some races, like the New York City Marathon, have these pads at several locations along the route in case there is ever concern about whether a runner actually ran the entire route.

Once you are running, make sure you are going at the pace that's best for you. It's easy to get pulled along with the crowd, especially with all the excitement in the air. But if you go out too strong in the start, you may not have the energy to keep up a good pace for the remainder of the race. Don't worry about people passing you; focus on yourself.

Two ways of getting through a difficult race are to associate and dissociate. I've gone over the value of dissociating in previous chapters, but association is another valuable method of mentally coping with a run. You associate by focusing entirely on what you are doing and what is going on specifically in the race. Think about how your legs are moving, focus on your pace, analyze your gait, keep your eye on the bend up ahead, and so forth.

Once you near the finish line, feel free to kick it up a notch and pick up your speed. After you cross that finish line, you'll be glad you did. The last few minutes of a race can be painful, no matter what the distance, but after you've stopped running and the discomfort subsides, you'll wonder what your time would have been if you'd given the last leg your absolute best. This is where knowing where the finish line is comes in very handy.

Make sure you get your medal or T-shirt. It's also advisable to plan a meeting spot with your friends and loved ones beforehand—race scenes can be pretty harried.

AFTER THE RACE

Take time to bask in the glory of what you have just accomplished. You've achieved a major goal; you should give yourself some time to think about that fact and all the hard work it took to get you there. I have often regretted leaving the race site too early. After a race you are on a high and may not realize until later that sitting around in a festival environment designed to celebrate what you and thousands of other people have just done is where you ought to be, not home on the couch where your tired legs told you to be. Take time; drink it all in. I also like to reward myself after every race somehow—usually with barbecue-flavored Fritos. While the glory and ego boost are great reward, any good celebration needs some tasty chow!

RACING FOR LIFE

Once you've run a race, you've crossed over into the running community and you can never go back—or at least, it's hard to. Once you pinned a race bib up on your pegboard, it's impossible to look at it and not think about how great you felt. And it's hard to not keep up with your running once you've "sealed" it with a race. I have every bib from every race I've ever run hanging on a wall in my office. I write down on the bib the date of the race, my time, and where the race took place so I can always remember that day. Most of the bibs are crumpled and stained by sweat or rain, but they are among my most treasured possessions. They tell the tale of my running career, which began with a 67-minute 10K in 1993.

OTHER RACING TIPS

✔ Wear shoes that have already been broken in.
✔ Spread Vaseline on any areas prone to chafing.
✔ Don't worry about being the last to finish; chances are you won't be.

- ✔ Wear clothing that you have worn before to avoid discomfort.
- ✔ Dress so that you will remain cool throughout the run.
- ✔ Carry your own water bottle to ensure you get enough water.
- ✔ Wear a hat to keep sun and rain out of your eyes.
- ✔ Carry Power Gels or other endurance foods for half- and full marathons.
- ✔ Apply sunscreen to avoid getting sunburn.
- ✔ Relax!

CHAPTER SIXTEEN

THE WEATHER

Just because it's –25 with the windchill doesn't mean you can't go for your run! You may think that that's crazy, but in fact, not only is it safe, but those blustery, gray days are sometimes the days you need your run the most. The same goes for those hot, hazy days of summer that leave many new runners wondering if they shouldn't hang up their sneakers for a few weeks. While there are days in both summer and winter when it won't be safe to go for a run, the truth is, in most of North America, those days can be counted on one hand each year. If you are using your runs to help take control of your emotional life, it would be a shame to let the weather stand in your way. To get the full effects of running in your life, you must run year-round. While there are always indoor tracks and treadmills, I suggest learning to brave the elements so that you'll never have an excuse like "they close at 8 P.M." That said, however, if you aren't dressed appropriately, cold, wet, and really hot days can be awful for runs. Additionally, there are some precautions that you must take to ensure that you are safe in extreme weather conditions. While I hate to admit it, there are in fact weather conditions that are not safe for running. It's critical that you learn the ins and outs of running in extreme temperatures to ensure you remain safe, and happy, at all times.

WINTER RUNNING

I live in the Great White North and I can count on two hands how many times I've had to put off running because of winter weather. The truth is, wintertime is a much more pleasant time of year to run. The cooler temperatures keep your head cool, making the run more enjoyable. It's amazing how much of the discomfort of running stems from overheating. You may be thinking at this point that you'll be freezing your buns off in the winter instead. But the truth is, you break a sweat running no matter how cold it is outside. And I can't tell you how invigorating it is to break a sweat in subzero weather! Despite what some people think, your throat and lungs will not freeze from running in the winter. It may feel uncomfortable at first, but once you warm up, and if you are dressed properly, you'll feel fine.

As I outlined in chapter 9, you really want to be wearing a synthetic fabric that will wick the moisture away from your body when you are running in cold weather. Cotton will hold that moisture next to your skin, and you'll be quite uncomfortable in no time. Also remember that you should be dressing for weather 20 degrees F (11 degrees C) warmer than it actually is outside. You don't want to overdress. However, don't forget about the windchill. Find out how cold the wind is making it feel outside, then base what you are going to wear on that temperature. Don't forget to cover your head; 40 percent of your body heat escapes through your head.

Winter Running Tips

- ✔ Adjust training for temperature and snowfall.
- ✔ Shorten your stride on ice.
- ✔ Do a warm-up before you go.
- ✔ Carry a coin in case you run into trouble.
- ✔ Don't do speedwork.
- ✔ Drink plenty of water.
- ✔ Stretch; no sudden moves.
- ✔ Put sheet metal screws in the bottoms of your shoes; avoid ice patches.
- ✔ Wear a balaclava.
- ✔ Cover exposed skin with Vaseline.

WINDCHILL

	ACTUAL AIR TEMPERATURE (°F)								
CALM	40	30	20	10	0	-10	-20	-30	-40
WIND SPEED (M.P.H)	**EQUIVALENT CHILL TEMPERATURE**								
5	35	25	15	5	-5	-15	-25	-35	-45
10	30	15	5	-10	-20	-35	-45	-60	-70
15	25	10	-5	-20	-30	-45	-60	-70	-85
20	20	5	-10	-25	-35	-50	-65	-80	-95
25	15	0	-15	-30	-45	-60	-75	-90	-105
30	10	0	-20	-30	-50	-65	-80	-95	-110
35	10	-5	-20	-35	-50	-65	-80	-100	-115
40	10	-5	-20	-35	-55	-70	-85	-100	-115

	ACTUAL AIR TEMPERATURE (°C)								
CALM	4	-1	-7	-12	-18	-23	-29	-34	-40
WIND SPEED (KM/H)	**EQUIVALENT CHILL TEMPERATURE**								
8	2	-4	-9	-15	-21	-26	-32	-37	-43
16	-1	-9	-15	-23	-29	-37	-43	-51	-57
24	-4	-12	-21	-29	-34	-43	-51	-57	-65
32	-7	-15	-23	-32	-37	-46	-54	-62	-71
40	-9	-18	-26	-34	-46	-51	-59	-68	-76
48	-12	-18	-29	-34	-46	-54	-62	-71	-79
56	-12	-21	-29	-37	-46	-54	-62	-73	-82
64	-12	-21	-29	-37	-48	-57	-65	-73	-82

APPARENT TEMPERATURE	RISK OF FROSTBITE
Above 20°F/30°C	Little danger
–20 to –70°F/–30 to –57°C	Increasing danger—exposed flesh may freeze within 1 minute
Below–70°F/–57°C	Great danger—exposed flesh may freeze within 30 seconds

Note: winds above 40 m.p.h./64 km/h have little additional effect.

✔ Get out of damp clothes fast.
✔ Run in groups for safety.

When and Where

In colder weather you may want to put some extra thought into when and where you run. It gets dark earlier in the wintertime, so you may have to move your runs to a different time of day. Additionally, it's a good idea to check the direction of the wind. You might want to run the first half of your run into the wind, so that it will be at your back on the way back home. Or you may choose to run in a loop; this will allow you to easily turn back if the weather gets too rough or you run into trouble.

Frostbite

Frostbite occurs when your skin is exposed to extreme cold temperatures. Your nose, cheeks, ears, toes, and fingers are most at risk. Symptoms of frostbite include numbing of the skin, reddening of the skin, shivering, loss of hand control, and drowsiness. More advanced frostbite can result in skin turning blotchy and gray, then turning white. Anyone suffering from frostbite should get out of the cold immediately, wrap the injured body part in wet, warm cloths or in warm (not hot) water, and seek medical attention.

Hypothermia

Hypothermia is when your body's core temperature drops below a normal range and your metabolic processes slow down. There is fluid loss; your pulse rate drops. Symptoms of hypothermia include incoherence, slurred speech, poor coordination, and clumsiness. If you suspect you are suffering from hypothermia, it's critical that you get someplace dry and warm quickly and seek medical advice.

SUMMER RUNNING

While summer running can be unpleasant if you are not dressed properly, it can be positively dangerous if you haven't taken a few precautions. It's important to wear clothing that will keep your body as cool as possible and to hydrate as well as you can. On a hot day you want to be drinking water before, during, and after your runs. When you know you will be going for a run later in the day, start hydrating early. Your body cools itself by sweating. But the more water you lose through sweating, the harder it is for your body to cool itself down. Your organs also need to be moist to stay cool, so continually replenish your fluids.

Summer Running Tips

- ✔ Drink lots of water.
- ✔ Don't do speedwork or hills.
- ✔ Run during the coolest times of day.
- ✔ Bring water for longer runs.
- ✔ Run in shade.
- ✔ Stop running if you feel lightheaded.
- ✔ Wear a white hat.
- ✔ Wet your hair before you go.
- ✔ Limit alcohol and caffeinated beverages such as coffee and tea.
- ✔ Watch out for goosebumps, paleness, and suddenly slowing down.

Heat Exhaustion and Heatstroke

Symptoms of heat exhaustion or heatstroke include hold and cold flashes, cold skin, dizziness, a decrease in perspiration, headache, confusion, and disorientation. These conditions can be fatal, so it's crucial that you get out of the sun and get help immediately.

Humidity

When there's a lot of moisture in the air, your body can't cool itself down properly because the moisture on your skin won't evaporate. Therefore, you can overheat a lot faster on humid days than on days when the air is dry. Just as with the windchill in the winter, you should check the Humidex to determine just how hot outside it really feels. You choice of what to wear should be based on this reading, not what the thermometer says.

HEAT INDEX

	AIR TEMPERATURE (°F)										
	70	75	80	85	90	95	100	105	110	115	120
RELATIVE HUMIDITY	**APPARENT TEMPERATURE**										
0%	64	69	73	78	83	87	91	95	99	103	107
10%	65	70	75	80	85	90	95	100	105	113	115
20%	66	72	77	82	87	93	99	105	112	120	130
30%	67	73	78	84	90	96	104	113	123	135	148
40%	68	74	79	86	93	101	110	123	137	151	
50%	69	75	81	88	96	107	120	135	150		
60%	70	76	82	90	100	114	132	149			
70%	70	77	85	93	106	124	144				
80%	71	78	86	97	113	136					
90%	71	79	88	102	122						
100%	72	80	91	106							

	AIR TEMPERATURE (°c)										
	21.0	23.8	26.6	29.4	32.2	35.0	37.7	40.5	43.3	46.1	48.8
RELATIVE HUMIDITY	**APPARENT TEMPERATURE**										
0%	17.0	20.5	22.7	25.5	28.3	30.5	32.8	35.0	37.2	39.4	41.0
10%	17.0	21.0	23.8	26.6	29.4	32.2	35.0	37.7	40.5	43.8	46.6
20%	18.8	22.2	35.0	27.7	30.5	33.8	37.2	40.5	44.4	48.8	54.4
30%	19.4	22.7	25.5	28.8	32.2	35.5	40.0	45.0	50.5	57.2	64.4
40%	20.0	23.8	26.1	30.0	33.8	39.3	43.3	50.5	58.3	66.1	
50%	20.5	23.8	27.2	31.1	35.5	41.6	48.8	57.2	65.5		
60%	21.0	24.4	27.7	32.2	37.7	45.5	55.5	65.0			
70%	21.0	25.0	29.4	33.8	41.1	51.1	62.2				
80%	21.5	25.5	30.0	36.1	45.0	57.7					
90%	21.5	26.1	31.1	38.8	50.0						
100%	22.2	26.6	32.9	42.2							

APPARENT TEMPERATURE	RISK FROM PROLONGED EXERCISE OR EXPOSURE
64-90°F/17.0-32.2°C	Fatigue, dehydration possible
90-105°F/32.2-40.5°C	Heat cramps or heat exhaustion possible
105-130°F/40.5-54.4°C	Heat cramps or heat exhaustion likely; heatstroke possible
130° F/54.4°C and up	Heatstroke highly likely

RUNNING IN THE RAIN

Rainstorms are my favorite weather to run in. Early-spring downpours may be a little on the cold side, but spring or summer showers are ideal. You need a hat with a brim to avoid having your salty sweat run into your eyes; watch your footing, too, as the wet pavement can be slick. If you can't avoid puddles in weather like this, you might want to try putting small plastic bags over your socks before putting on your shoes. Secured with an elastic band around the ankle, these makeshift foot protectors will keep your feet warm and dry.

Lightning and hailstorms are two conditions in which I advise against going out for a run. Hail pellets have been known to cause head injuries; also, drivers may not be able to see or maneuver their cars as safely as they can in normal circumstances. Lightning, meanwhile, has been known to strike the tallest things in a clearing—and runners on a roadway might sometimes fit that bill. So in either of these conditions, I'd say save your run for another day or head for the treadmill.

While fall and spring are no doubt the best running seasons, with a few tricks up your sleeve and some perseverance, there's no reason you can't enjoy your outdoor runs year-round. When you depend on those escapes from the house for your emotional health, it will be worth braving some ice and humidity.

CHAPTER SEVENTEEN

PREGNANCY AND RUNNING

Despite common belief, pregnancy is not necessarily a reason to stop running. In fact, running can actually be a way to take back control of your life when things are hormonally spinning out of control. I hope to be able to run through all of my pregnancies, as many, many women before me have done. To be honest, I can't imagine having to go through something so emotionally and physically challenging without my trusty coping mechanism.

But women cannot always continue to run during pregnancy as they did before. And in some cases, women cannot continue to run at all. There has been a great deal of research into the risks associated with continued exercise during pregnancy, and so far it has shown that women can continue to exercise moderately through their pregnancy. Many studies have also shown the marked benefits, physical and mental, for both mother and baby. However, there are some guidelines that women must follow if they chose to continue running through pregnancy. First, every woman should start by talking with her doctor. Some doctors are not aware of the new research showing how safe running can be, so you may have to interview a few physicians to find someone who is open to guiding you down this road.

IS IT SAFE?

When women are pregnant, our respiratory, cardiovascular, and thermoregulatory systems are forced to work harder than usual. This is also the case when we run. So when you ask your body to do both at one time, these systems are really put to the test. This is the root of a lot of the concern about running and exercising through pregnancy. If your blood is being diverted to your muscles, is blood flow being diverted away from the fetus? If you are breathing harder, is that making it harder for the baby to breathe? And finally, if your body temperature goes up from exercising, can that hurt the baby? These and other concerns have been addressed in a number of scientific studies over the years, which have all concluded that exercising through pregnancy is safe with a few precautions.

In a study conducted in 1983, the Melpomene Institute found that women and babies tolerate physical activity through pregnancy very well. In fact, the institute says exercise is a healthy adjunct to a healthy pregnancy. However, research has not provided a clear picture of what level of exercise is dangerous. The American College of Obstetricians and Gynecologists had at one time released guidelines directing women to not exceed 140 heartbeats per minute. Then in February 1994, following more updated studies, the ACOG lifted its restriction on intensity and duration of exercise during pregnancy. James Clapp III, M.D., author of *Exercising Through Your Pregnancy* and a leading expert in this area, says you can safely exercise for an hour. Also, there is no evidence that women who are used to exercising for two hours or more can't continue. What all experts do agree on, however, is that you must get permission from your OB before exercising and ask her to help design an appropriate program. It's also important to know that no studies have shown a greater rate of early delivery in women who exercise.

Blood-Flow Concerns

While exercise does redirect blood flow to our muscles during exercise, researchers say our bodies make adjustments to ensure the fetus gets enough blood too. Cardiac output increases by an estimated 30 to 50 percent, and blood volumes expand by 35 to 45 percent during pregnancy, experts say. Therefore, it's unlikely moderate running could cause insufficient blood flow to the fetus.

Body Temperature Concerns

Studies on animals have shown that high body temperatures can damage a fetus, but no such evidence exists for humans. Doctors do, however, fear that if a woman's body temperature goes above 103 degrees F in the first 30 to 50 days of pregnancy, birth defects are possible. This fear stems from the fact that the neural tube, which later becomes the spinal cord, is very sensitive to heat. But just as the body adjusts during pregnancy to accommodate the increased blood-flow needs, the body's temperature regulation abilities also improve. Also, with the increased body weight, pregnant women improve their capacity for heat storage and can therefore generate 20 percent more heat without raising their temperature, says Dr. Clapp. While active woman are also thought to be better at keeping their bodies cool to begin with, doctors do advise pregnant women to be careful about letting their body temperature rise too high. It's recommended that a pregnant woman's body temperature not exceed 102 degrees F. Pregnant runners should be sure to dress appropriately, take it easy, not run in particularly hot conditions, and drink lots of water.

Birth Weight

Another area of concern has been the birth weight of runners' babies. While runners' babies do tend to weigh less than the average baby, their weights remain in a healthy range. Runners' babies have an average body fat of 10 percent versus the 15 percent average.

LIMITATIONS

The American College of Obstetrics and Gynecology outlines some very specific conditions that will limit or prevent exercise during pregnancy altogether:

- ✔ Toxemia or pregnancy-induced high blood pressure
- ✔ Vaginal bleeding
- ✔ Pre-term labor or a history of it
- ✔ Intrauterine growth retardation or poor growth of fetus
- ✔ Twins
- ✔ Heart disease
- ✔ Active thyroids

Source: "Exercise during pregnancy and the post-partum period," Technical Bulletin 189, American College of Obstetricians and Gynecologists, Washington D.C., 1994.

PAIN AND FATIGUE

While studies have shown that in most pregnancies women are able to continue running, sometimes there are other issues in play. Some women may find that they are just too tired to keep up with their running, or may find it uncomfortable or even painful past a certain point, says Judy Mahle Lutter of the Melpomene Institute. "It varies greatly from woman to woman. A lot of women who expect to be able to run through their pregnancies are often quite discouraged to find it's just uncomfortable. I think it's very important to support this eventuality. I know women who have run to the delivery room . . . but that's not going to be all women."

EMOTIONAL AND PHYSICAL HEALTH BENEFITS

The evidence of the physical and emotional health benefits of exercise during pregnancy for both mother and baby is extensive. Moms can expect exercising through pregnancy to bring improved cardiovascular function, limited weight gain and fat retention, improved attitude and mental state, easier and less complicated labor, quick recovery from delivery, and less nausea, fatigue, and leg cramps. A study conducted at the University of Melbourne in 2000 on the body image and psychological well-being of pregnant women showed that exercisers had reduced frequency of anxiety and insomnia along with a higher level of psychological well-being and better body image. Therefore, experts say women should be encouraged to maintain their pre-pregnancy activity level.

As for the baby, science has shown that a mother's exercise during gestation decreases the growth of the fetus's fat organ and improves stress tolerance. Studies have also shown that the babies of women who exercise have advanced neurobehavioral maturation, have slightly better neurodevelopmental outcome, and are leaner at five years old than children born to mothers who did not exercise. While I suspect these last findings may be more a result of what type of woman would choose to continue exercising through pregnancy, such outcomes prove women can exercise through pregnancy without impeding the growth of the fetus.

Weight Gain

The baby's health aside, weight gain is a major area of concern for women who become pregnant. Gaining weight is a natural part of any healthy pregnancy, but many women develop body image concerns as a result. This can be a contributing factor in pregnancy depression and anxiety. Running and other forms of aerobic exercise can help curb this by limiting the amount of weight women gain during pregnancy. The recommended weight gain for women during their pregnancy is between 25 and 40 pounds. A study conducted by the Melpomene Institute found that the average weight gain for runners during pregnancy was 25 pounds, versus 31 pounds for nonrunners. Therefore, most women who run through their pregnancy can expect to stay closer to the low end of the healthy weight gain range during their pregnancy.

Delivery

There are conflicting reports on whether or not women who exercise experience easier and less complicated deliveries than women who don't. Some studies have reported that women who stayed fit during pregnancy had elevated levels of beta-endorphin during labor and delivery, which is believed to reduce their pain perception. Meanwhile, others say exercise can't shorten or lesson pain of labor but can help women "frame their pain." No data exists to show exercisers have fewer cesareans or use fewer drugs during delivery, although many doctors report anecdotal evidence of active women having easier deliveries.

GUIDELINES FOR RUNNING THROUGH PREGNANCY

While it is safe for women having a healthy pregnancy to continue their pre-pregnancy level of activity, there are a number of guidelines pregnant exercisers should follow. It's also important to note that women who did not exercise prior to pregnancy should not start until the second trimester, and again, under the supervision of a doctor. These women also will not be able to do as much during their pregnancy as their counterparts who have always been active.

Other Guidelines

- ✔ Keep exercise in the mild to moderate range.
- ✔ Exercising three times weekly is preferable to intermittent exercise.
- ✔ Avoid anything that could cause any kind of abdominal trauma.
- ✔ Avoid exercise on your back after the first trimester.
- ✔ Stop immediately if you are lightheaded or can't catch your breath.
- ✔ Avoid standing in one spot for long periods.
- ✔ Don't exercise to exhaustion.
- ✔ Avoid exercises that could cause you to lose balance.
- ✔ Eat properly and increase your intake by 300 calories per day.
- ✔ To avoid overheating, drink plenty of fluids, dress appropriately, and exercise in cool conditions.

Pregnancy Exercise Tips

- ✔ Wear maternity gear (elastic maternity belts).
- ✔ Schedule runs when you won't be tired.
- ✔ Consider wearing a heart rate monitor.
- ✔ Make sure your urine is pale yellow to avoid dehydration.

- ✔ Make sure you can talk during your runs.
- ✔ Keep workouts to 25 to 45 minutes.
- ✔ Carry a cell phone in case anything goes wrong.
- ✔ Listen to your body.
- ✔ Buy a good support bra.
- ✔ Stop racing, speedwork, or long, hard runs.
- ✔ Drink at least 8 to 12 glasses of water daily.

What to Wear

Dressing appropriately is key to keeping your body cool. Again, remember to dress for weather that is 20 degrees F (11degrees C) warmer than it actually is outside. You want to keep cool, so cover your head with a white hat, wear lightweight sports fabrics, and run in the shade. Later in the pregnancy, many runners find they need some abdominal support due to tension in the ligaments supporting the uterus. A pregnancy belt can help by holding the baby tight to your body. Bike shorts can have the same effect. Our breasts also increase in size during pregnancy, so many women who have never had to think about a support bra may suddenly find themselves in need of more support. There are a number of good sport bras on the market that can provide comfort to women of any chest size.

Stretching

During pregnancy, our bodies release relaxin, a chemical that makes our joints and ligaments looser but also makes us more vulnerable to injury. Proper stretching is a good way to help avoid such injuries. As with other exercise, however, there are some restrictions pregnant women should be aware of. There are a number of good books on stretches for pregnant women.

POSTPARTUM RUNNING

Every woman has to make her own decision about when it is time for her to start running again after delivery. Experts recommend waiting two to six weeks before starting back. Still, some women have jumped back on the horse immediately after delivery without any problems. A study of a 34-year-old distance runner who started a 16-week marathon training program immediately after giving birth showed that well-trained women can participate in vigorous activity soon after pregnancy. As a competitive athlete, this woman may have had a lot of incentive to get back into such intense training so quickly. Most women don't and would be wise to take some time to rest, recuperate from both the pregnancy and delivery, and get to know their child.

The Melpomene Institute has issued the following guidelines for exercising after having a baby:

- ✔ If you had an episiotomy, wait until all soreness is gone.
- ✔ If you're bleeding heavily, or your blood is bright red, wait.
- ✔ Be aware of continuing joint elasticity.
- ✔ Fatigue is common.
- ✔ Drink a lot of water if you are nursing.
- ✔ Don't forget to continue to support your breasts.
- ✔ Use Kegel exercises for bladder incontinence.
- ✔ Watch your posture to avoid back pain.
- ✔ Make sure you warm up before working out.
- ✔ Eat well.

ANTEPARTUM AND POSTPARTUM BLUES

With one in ten pregnant women suffering from depression during pregnancy and up to 85 percent of new mothers suffering from postpartum depression, it's clear mental health is a major issue during and after pregnancy. Just as exercise has been proven to combat depression, stress, and anxiety at other times in our lives, workouts can be a valuable weapon against depression during and after pregnancy. Fluctuating moods, tearfulness, confusion, and insomnia are among the many symptoms of these conditions and can make an already challenging life situation even more difficult. Getting back into your fitness regime as soon as you can after delivery can help you feel like yourself again while giving you some time to yourself, something most new mothers could use more of.

Judy Mahle Lutter says her studies at the Melpomene Institute have shown that the emotional health benefits of running are often demonstrated the most during the postpartum period. "Postpregnancy running can be a real boon," she notes. "If women can run, it tends to alleviate their symptoms. You are the caretaker for this young child and often what falls out of the mix is taking time for yourself." Hitting the road for a run can give women those few minutes of solace they may need now more than ever.

BREAST-FEEDING

There has been a great deal of study into whether or not exercise affects the quality or quantity of breast milk. One study found that babies did not like the taste of breast milk taken from their mothers after they exercised. Unfortunately, that study was tainted by the fact that those children were breast-fed, yet were given the test milk with a bottle. Many breast-fed babies show disinterest in bottles. While studies have shown that there is an increased amount of lactic acid, a by-product of exercise, found in the breast milk of women who exercise, experts have concluded that babies can't tell the difference and that exercise does not affect quality or quantity of milk. However, mothers may want to consider feeding their children before they run. They should also be careful to keep their weight in a healthy range and to eat and drink well.

STEPHANIE'S STORY: ON SURVIVING PREGNANCY AND BEYOND

Stephanie Nilsson, 24, Sweden

Moving to a new country, graduating from college, learning a new language, and giving birth to premature twins all within the same nine-month period, Stephanie Nilsson knows a thing or two about stress. Having used running as a stress reliever before her pregnancy, she switched to pool running and cycling after she found out she was pregnant with twins. Throughout her pregnancy and especially during her postpartum period, Stephanie says running saved her sanity. Here's her story:

The only thing in my life that had not changed was my name—although I was thinking of changing it to "One-stressed-out-mamma." It was the most interesting nine months of my life. However, the stress did not decrease after the babies were born, and we were settled in our new home. Emma and Sebastian made their grand entry two months early, and together we spent a month in the hospital's neonatal unit. The stress only began to decrease when everyone was home safe, and we began life's journey as a family.

I had just trained to the 10-mile mark when I found out I was pregnant. The news was a wonderful surprise to my husband and me. I continued to run lesser distances at the okay of my physician until the ultrasound technician said to us, "Here is your precious baby . . . and here is your other one." I was shocked, ecstatic, but worried that running would not be the best form of exercise for a twin pregnancy. The three of us changed to water aerobics at our local university! Whenever I would jog in the water the babies would do flipflops in excitement. Exercising was a conscious decision I made for the health of my babies and as a stress reducer to me. I knew big changes were coming, and I was going to face them in the best mental and physical shape for the health of my unborn twins.

During the time I found out I was pregnant, I was also finishing my student teaching. This is another name that should be changed; student teaching *should become, "don't do anything to mess it up because your whole future depends on the last three months of the four years you spent in college." I was placed in a school where three of the five student teachers were kicked out of the program. Yep, I needed a stress reducer. Running in the pool was just the thing. I was able to use the time to imagine what my babies were doing at that very moment, or if they would have my big ears, or my husband's slightly less big ears. I cleared my mind and concentrated on what my body was saying, rather than on outside stimulants. It was a time to feel special, and strong, rather than frumpy and out of control.*

Two days after the last final of my undergraduate career, when I was six months pregnant, I moved to Sweden from the United States.

We settled into our new home, and I continued to exercise by riding my bike all over town. I enrolled in Swedish lessons and took life as it came, for a little while. My doctor told me I had to slow down because the babies looked like they were going to come early. Two weeks later, I was walking the dogs with my husband and was on the way home when my water broke. Thirteen hours later my daughter decided to stick her foot out in front of her brother, blocking his passage. It was off to have a C-section.

The babies were two months early, but very healthy. Because they were so young, they had to be tube-fed breast milk, and had to stay in the hospital for a month. Everything was going great with them, but I was still stressed with the situation. Instead of getting out and exercising, I ate! I ate constantly for the next three months, and put on 20 more pounds than I weighed after giving birth. During the fourth month I woke up when I realized that my maternity pants were getting tight! I packed the babies up and took them to the gym. By this time, it was January in Sweden and about –20 degrees Celsius. We would go the warm gym and the babies would sleep with ear protectors on while I did a step or body pump aerobics class. The weight was beginning to come off, slowly.

When spring and my Baby Jogger arrived, we got out and hit the trails. Nothing could compare to the feeling I had! We have a beautiful trail around the lake we like to run. After the turmoil of the move and the early delivery, it was nice to be in control of something. I could control my running. My mind could relax, and the stress of the daily care of twins eased. I was becoming the mother I wanted to be, because running relaxed me enough to be there both mentally and physically for my family. Gradually, we increased our mileage and the weight began to fly off. I did not diet a single day; I only exercised. Being overweight for the first time in my life scared and surprised me. I felt trapped in this foreign form. It was the first time I could not move as I wanted, and I could not believe I had let myself get to this powerless point.

Running has not only given me back my mind and body; it is also a gift to my children. I want them to see exercise as something wonderful, not as a chore to keep down their weight. I want them to have fun, to run and play! I do not want them to feel trapped in a body that cannot move. I have now lost 21 of the 40 pounds I want to lose. I am finally participating in life with my family instead of warming the bench as everyone else plays.

Becky Yeager, 35, Logan, Utah

Becky Yeager says she started running after the birth of her second daughter two and a half years ago in an effort to keep a hold of her sanity. As a wildlife biologist who works from home, Becky Yeager has at times found balancing work and motherhood a true struggle. But by taking the time to strap her kids into a Burley Cart (a cycling cart converted into a sports jogger) and head out for regular 10 -mile runs, Yeager says she has again found emotional balance.

I shudder to think what my mental condition would be without running. As a mother of two- and three-year old girls, like most moms, I have days when I reach my tolerance level by 8:00 A.M. By the third milk spill and the second "I want cookies for breakfast," I'm ready to head out the door. Don't get me wrong, my kids are cute. But sometimes being a mom wears one down faster than a Popsicle on a hot summer day. This mom needs an outlet to release the negative energy that builds with each unauthorized haircut or off-the-paper, on-the-wall art project. Not only did running allow me to put the nitpicking and rule-making aside temporarily, but it allowed me to refocus on the greatest opportunity in life, being a mom. Regardless of my kids' temperaments during my runs, I feel like I've accomplished something when I arrive home. As a mom, I often feel unrewarded for my day-to-day tasks. Unrecognized, unappreciated, disrespected . . . .I could go on. Running, on the other hand, has allowed me to validate myself. To take control of those feelings and put them in perspective. It's allowed me to be proud of myself. That pride somehow spills over to all aspects of my life. In the last two and a half years, I've run three marathons and several 15K and placed (in the winner's circle) in all of them. Surprisingly, the trophies have been such a small part of the accomplishment. It's reaching my goals that has been so important to my sense of self-worth. More importantly, I am starting to realize what a valuable lesson this is to my children. I see them setting goals and working hard to reach those goals. And I love the fact that they have a happy, confident mom as a role model.

These runs have been invaluable to my physical and mental health, and possibly that of my children. As a bonus, the runs have carried me to several marathons. After all, running a marathon parallels child-rearing. I've even brought home a few trophies (who knew that a cart could be used as a training tool?). In the big picture, though, I don't run for the competition—I run for my sanity.

CHAPTER EIGHTEEN

Get Even Stronger

While running can in so many ways make both your mind and body stronger, it is a sport that can leave various body parts unchallenged. As we all know, running predominantly involves use of our lower bodies, leaving our arms, stomachs, backs, chests, and various other body parts far less developed. In order to make up for these imbalances and keep our entire body strong, it's a good idea to throw a few other exercises into the mix. Cross-training, or participating in another sport that complements running, is one great way to do that. Lifting weights is another very effective method of targeting those weaker muscles. You can even fill in those gaps in your overall body fitness with some floor work that you can do sitting in front of the television. Whichever your choice, picking a strengthening routine can be one of the best ways to improve your running, keep you fit to run, and spice up your regimen.

CROSS-TRAINING

Participating in another sport that complements your running can not only make you a stronger runner, but also help you avoid injury. It can give you a way to stay fit when you are injured and help keep you motivated. Cross-training can also add some variety to your workout routine when it gets a little repetitious. Adding other sports to your week can improve your muscle flexibility and continue to build on your cardiovascular development. When deciding on other sports to use for cross-training, pick something that mimics the motions of running—although not exactly. That way, you not only strengthen the muscles used in running but also work on some of those muscles that aren't used to the same extent when you are out for a run. An example of this would be cycling. It's important that you choose a cross-training sport that does not have the same weight-bearing nature as running has. For instance, high-impact aerobic classes are probably not your best choice. After spending hours a week pounding the pavement running, you should try to give your legs, hips, and feet a rest.

Cycling

Riding a bike is one of the best forms of cross-training for runners. The leg-turnover motion is much like running, strengthening many of the same muscles but in a different way, putting them to a new test. This turnover motion can also translate into a faster turnover when you are running, improving your running speed. Also, on a bike there is no impact. This gives your lower body a chance to have a good workout without all that heavy pounding found with running. Cycling is a particularly good cross-training choice for injured runners. You can continue to build muscle, stamina, and cardio function while giving your injury a bit of a break. Cycling also gives a harder workout to your hamstrings, helping balance out strength disparity between the hamstrings and the quadriceps muscles (which are often stronger than hamstrings in runners).

Water Running

While not a well-known sport, water running is an ideal cross-training choice for runners because it exactly mimics running, but without the impact and in much cooler conditions. Minute for minute, water running gives you as good of a workout as you would get out on the road. The sport requires a flotation belt to keep you from sinking, with the option of hand and foot devices to make movement easier. Some people stride across the length of the pool, others stay put, running "on the spot." Once you are in the pool, with your flotation belt on, you simply start to "run" in the water. This involves pumping your legs in the same turnover motion you would use on the road. Meanwhile, pump your arms forward and back to help stay afloat. You will need to use your hands to help pull you forward if you choose to go across the length of the pool. It's best to water run in water that is deeper than you are tall, so the bottom of the pool does not interfere with your motion. Many people find the foot and hand devices make this workout more enjoyable since they are built to help you pull yourself through the water (almost liked having webbed hands and feet).

This is an ideal choice for injured runners because not only can it keep you running when you are hurt, but the cold water can help keep the swelling down in injured areas. One added bonus of water running is the fact that your arms get a better workout than they do on the road. The resistance of the water also adds to the sport's benefits. Water running can improve your running form and work out a number of other muscles that don't normally get a solid workout.

Cross-Country Skiing

While I believe no amount of snow on the ground is reason to not run, there is one sport that might sometimes be worth hanging up the sneakers for. Cross-country skiing is another fabulous cross-training workout that provides a real challenge to your muscles and cardiovascular system without the impact of running. Cross-country skiers are among the fittest people in the world. Again, this sport mimics the body movements involved in running, but you don't have the weight of your body slamming down on your lower extremities. While building strength throughout your body, including your arms, cross-country skiing can also improve your flexibility and ultimately make you a stronger runner. Dashing through the snow in an orchard can also be a nice change of scenery.

In-Line Skating

While not mimicking the movements involved in running, in-line skating can build up other parts of your legs that aren't normally tested during a run. The inner and outer thighs are two areas that running doesn't really target. But on a pair of skates, those muscle areas can get a really good workout. Meanwhile, your calves, quadriceps, hamstrings, buttocks, and other muscles used in running also get a workout. And again, this sport is not high impact. However, there are some added safety concerns to consider before lacing up and rolling away. Helmets, wrist guards, and knee and elbow pads are all a must if you want to stay safe out there. While overuse injuries are our biggest fear as runners, a sudden, severe injury can mean taking several weeks off from our number one sport. So be safe.

Yoga

As outlined in chapter 10, yoga is a great way to strengthen the body and mind, making it an ideal cross-training sport. Strengthening and lengthening our muscles while working on our cardiovascular system, yoga is a fine workout. It does not, however, mimic running in any way and therefore can't be effectively used as a replacement for running in case of injury. But it can help us to avoid injury and give us a nice change of pace.

WEIGHT TRAINING

Adding weight lifting to your routine can not only make you a stronger runner but also helps you to fuel up for your runs. By building and training our muscles, we give our bodies more storage space to hold glycogen, the fuel our bodies use to run. With weights we can also target some of those muscle groups that get ignored during our runs—for instance, our arms. For runners, the idea is not to gain bulky muscles. For our purposes, we want long, lean, supple muscles. The best way to accomplish this is not to load up on as much weight as you can lift. Instead, you should do many repeats at a low weight—say, three sets of 25 repeats at a weight that is more than comfortable on the first lift.

Biceps

Using comfortable hand weights, lower your arms to your sides with your palms facing forward. Bend your elbows gently and slowly raise the weights until they almost touch your shoulders. Then slowly lower them to the starting position. Repeat 15 to 20 times and work up from there.

Triceps

With hand weights securely in your hands, raise both arms up beside your ears and bend your elbows so that the weights nearly touch your back. Slowly raise the weights until your arms are straight again. Repeat 10 to 15 times and work up from there.

Shoulders (Deltoids and Trapezius)

This is a great strength training option for women because it will increase the size and breadth of your shoulders, making your lower body more proportionate. Using hand weights, stand tall and place your arms at your sides. Slowly raise the weights until they are at shoulder level. Then lower your arms back to the starting position. Repeat 20 to 25 times and work up from there.

Chest

While modern science has made it possible to enhance our chest size with plastic, saline, and silicone, there is a healthier, more natural way to do it. Weight lifting that targets the pectoral muscles can build up the muscles behind our breasts. To pinpoint the pectoral muscles, lie on your back. With hand weights firmly in hand, bend your arms so that the lower portion of your arms is perpendicular to your body. Raise both arms until your arms are almost fully extended. Then lower your arms back to the starting position. Repeat 15 to 20 times.

Quadriceps

Sitting on the floor, bend one knee in front of you (foot on the floor) with your other leg extended. With the top of your leg facing the ceiling, slowly raise your leg as far off the ground as you can, hold it for a few seconds, then lower it back down. Repeat as many times as you can and work up from there.

Hamstrings

Lie on the floor on your stomach with your legs extended straight behind you. Keeping your leg straight, slowly raise it off the floor as far as you can, hold for a few seconds, then lower it back down to the ground. Repeat 25 times with each leg.

Calf Muscles

Using hand weights, stand with your feet shoulder-width apart. Holding your hands near your shoulders, slowly raise your heels off the ground and go up onto your toes. Then slowly lower yourself back to the floor. Start with 25 repeats.

FLOOR WORK

It's amazing how much of a workout you can get lying on the floor of your living room watching television. With just a few dozen repeats of a handful of exercises, you can isolate and significantly strengthen some of the hardest-to-improve areas of your body. Your abdomen, inner thighs, outer thighs, and hips are just some of the body parts you can improve with a little work on the floor.

The Ideal Ab Toner

Lying on your back with your head on the floor (or slightly elevated in your hands), hold your legs up in the air at a 90-degree angle. Your knees can be slightly bent. Don't worry about your lower back coming up off the floor. Now take a deep breath, let your abdomen fill up with air (and expand), then exhale while stretching one leg out in front of you, touching your toe to the ground. Hold it there for a few seconds. Then take a breath in, again allowing your stomach muscles to expand and fill with air, while you bring your leg back up to the starting position. Repeat with the other leg. Do an equal number of repeats with both legs. Start with 10 repeats, 5 on each side, and work up from there. This is one of the best ab flatteners around.

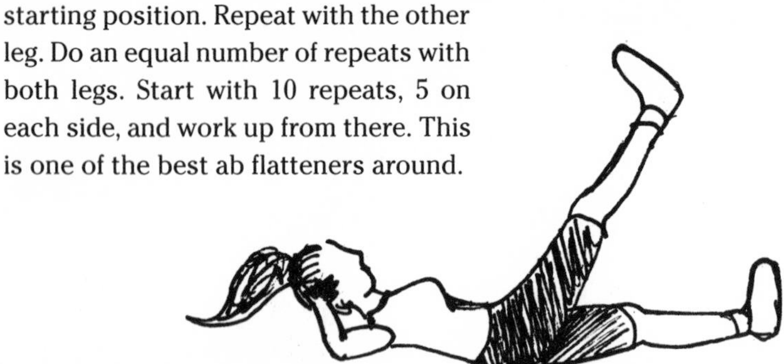

Inner Thighs

Lying on your side, propped up on your elbow, bend one knee, placing your foot on the floor in front of your straight leg. Then flex the foot of your straight leg and lift that leg toward the ceiling about 6 inches, before lowering it almost to the ground. Repeat 25 times, then switch and do the other leg. You can make this workout more difficult by putting 2- or 5-pound weights on your ankles, but be sure to work up to this level of effort.

Outer Thighs

Lying on your side, again propped up on one elbow, bend your lower leg at the knee. Then flex the foot of your straight leg and lift it about 12 inches toward the ceiling. Lower the leg again until it almost touches the ground and repeat 25 times. Do the same for the other leg. Again, this exercise can be done with leg weights.

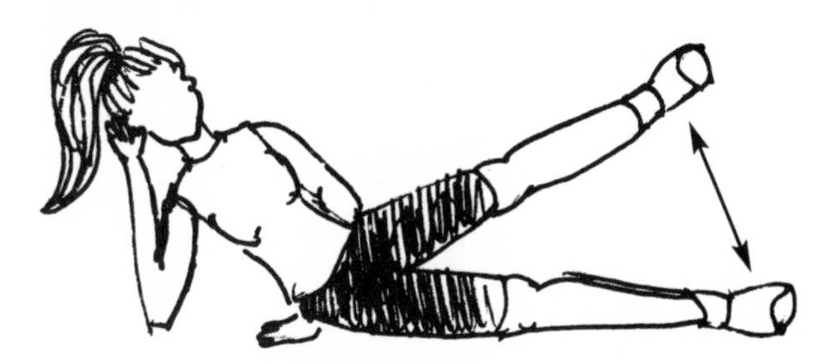

Thighs and Stomach

Lying on your back, propped up on both elbows, straighten both legs into the air. Slowly separate your legs, keeping your feet flexed, and lower them as far as you can. Then lift them back up to the starting position. Repeat this exercise 25 times and work up from there.

APPENDIX A

A Women's Running History

While women today are able to compete in all the same running events men enjoy, that hasn't always been the case. In fact, it's only been in the last 20 years that women runners have been treated as equals on the international running stage. The following is a chronological look at women's advancements in the sport, starting from a time when we were ironically encouraged to run like the boys.

Before 1500 B.C.

Women in ancient Egypt and Sparta are encouraged to participate in sports because it is believed that it will improve their reproductive capabilities.

776 B.C.

Women are forbidden from participating in or watching Olympic events. Any woman found breaking this rule faces being hurled off a cliff.

1800s

Women are strongly discouraged from participating in any activity at all mentally or physically challenging based on the idea that redirecting their energies might compromise their reproductive abilities.

1896 Olympics

A woman named Melpomene runs the marathon event as an unofficial entrant after being the first to be refused entry because of her sex. She completes the race in four and a half hours.

Early 1900s

The medical and sports communities in the Western world try to dissuade women from running for fear it will hurt their ability to have children or even cause their death.

1921

The first international governing body for women's athletics, Feminine Sportive Foundation Internationale (FSFI), is formed.

1922

The FSFI sponsors the first women's world championship, with the longest race just 1,000 meters.

1924

With several international meets already completed, the FSFI requests that the 1924 Olympics include events for women. The International Amateur Athletic Federation denies the request.

Great Britain's Violet Percy runs a marathon in 3 hours and 40 minutes.

1928

The International Amateur Athletic Foundation and the FSFI agree to work together to create four events at the 1928 Olympics. An 800-meter event is included. Lack of proper training for this event causes most of the entrants to collapse, reconfirming the belief that women shouldn't run longer distances.

1930

The National Amateur Athletic Federation petitions the International Olympic Committee president to eliminate women's track and field events from the 1932 Olympic Games. The petition is supported around the world.

1932

Despite being chosen as the first black women ever to be a part of the U.S. Olympic Team, Tidye Pickett and Louise Stokes are denied the opportunity to compete at the Los Angeles Olympics.

1948

A 30-year-old mother of two, Francina Blankers-Koen of Amsterdam, wins a record four Olympic gold medals in track and field (100 meters, 200 meters, 80 meters, and 4 X 100 relay).

1957

An organization called the Road Runners Club of America (RRCA) is formed specifically to promote long-distance running. Espousing the belief that women are capable of running long distances, the RRCA pressures race directors to allow women into their races, although the entries are unofficial at first.

1960

The women's 800-meter run is reinstated as an event at the Olympic Games.

1961

Julia Chase, a 19-year-old college student from New England, has her official entry refused in the Manchester, Connecticut, 5-mile road race.

1965

A women's 1.5-mile cross-country race in Seattle is the first to be recognized in the United States.

1966

Roberta Gibb Bingay sneaks into the Boston Marathon with no official entry and completes the race in 3 hours and 20 minutes.

1967

Katherine Switzer enters the Boston Marathon under the initial K. Switzer and is nearly physically dragged out of the race by race official Jock Semple. Switzer's football player boyfriend and coach help foil Semple's attempts and she finishes in 4 hours and 20 minutes.

The medical establishment reacts with shock when 13-year-old Canadian Maureen Wilton runs a marathon in Toronto in 3:15:22, the world's best time for a woman.

1970

In October the RRCA sponsors the American National Women's Marathon Championship.

1971

Beth Bohner brings the marathon record down to 2:55:22 at the New York City Marathon.

1972

Women compete in the 1,500-meter event at the Munich Olympics for the first time.

1974

The very first International Women's Marathon is held in West Germany, hosting 45 entrants.

1978

Partnering with Katherine Switzer, Avon organizes an international circuit of road races for women.

1982

The IAAF recognizes women's records in the 5,000- and 10,000-meter races.

1984

Women are finally allowed to compete in the marathon event at the Los Angeles Olympics.

1985

The women's world record for the marathon is broken by Ingrid Kristiansen in London with a time of 2:21:06—a record that will stand for 13 years.

1988

The women's 10,000-meter race is added to the Olympic Games in Seoul, Korea.

1992

Winning the 10,000-meter event at the Barcelona Olympics, Derartu Tulu of Ethiopia becomes the first African woman to win Olympic gold.

1996

At the Atlanta Olympics, the women's 5,000-meter event replaces the 3,000-meter event. Before this, women were only allowed to run the 3,000 meters, while men could run the 5,000 meters.

1998

Kenyan Tegla Loroupe sets a new women's world record for the marathon in the Rotterdam Marathon in the Netherlands, finishing with a time of 2:20:47.

2001

Naoko Takashashi of Japan becomes the first woman to break 2:20 minutes in the women's marathon in Berlin on September 30 with a time of 2:19:46.

Just one week later, on October 7, Catherine Ndereba of Kenya breaks that record with a time of 2:18:47 in Chicago.

APPENDIX B

Pace Charts

K PACE	1 MILE	5K	10K	15K	20K
2:55	4:42	14:35	29:10	43:45	58:20
3:00	4:50	15:00	30:00	45:00	1:00:00
3:05	4:58	15:25	30:50	46:15	1:01:40
3:10	5:06	15:50	31:40	47:30	1:03:20
3:15	5:14	16:15	32:30	48:45	1:05:00
3:20	5:22	16:40	33:20	50:00	1:06:40
3:25	5:30	17:05	34:10	51:15	1:08:20
3:30	5:38	17:30	35:00	52:30	1:10:00
3:35	5:46	17:55	35:50	53:45	1:11:00
3:40	5:54	18:20	36:40	55:00	1:13:20
3:45	6:02	18:45	37:30	56:15	1:15:00
3:50	6:10	19:10	38:20	57:30	1:16:40
3:55	6:18	19:35	39:10	58:45	1:18:20
4:00	6:26	20:00	40:00	1:00:00	1:20:00
4:05	6:34	20:25	40:50	1:01:15	1:21:40
4:10	6:42	20:50	41:40	1:02:30	1:23:20
4:15	6:50	21:15	42:30	1:03:45	1:25:00
4:20	6:58	21:40	43:20	1:05:00	1:26:40
4:25	7:06	22:05	44:10	1:06:15	1:28:20
4:30	7:14	22:30	45:00	1:07:30	1:30:00
4:35	7:23	22:55	45:50	1:08:45	1:31:40
4:40	7:31	23:20	46:40	1:10:00	1:33:20
4:45	7:39	23:45	47:30	1:11:15	1:35:00
4:50	7:47	24:10	48:20	1:12:30	1:36:40
4:55	7:55	24:35	49:10	1:13:45	1:38:20
5:00	8:03	25:00	50:00	1:15:00	1:40:00
5:05	8:11	25:25	50:50	1:16:15	1:41:40
5:10	8:19	25:50	51:40	1:17:30	1:43:20
5:15	8:27	26:15	52:30	1:18:45	1:45:00

21.1K	25K	30K	35K	40K	42.2K
1:01:32	1:12:55	1:27:30	1:42:05	1:56:40	2:03:04
1:03:17	1:15:00	1:30:00	1:45:00	2:00:00	2:06:35
1:05:03	1:17:05	1:32:30	1:47:55	2:03:20	2:10:16
1:06:28	1:19:10	1:35:00	1:50:50	2:06:40	2:13:37
1:08:34	1:21:15	1:37:30	1:53:45	2:10:00	2:17:08
1:10:19	1:23:20	1:40:00	1:56:40	2:13:20	2:20:39
1:12:05	1:25:25	1:42:25	1:59:35	2:16:40	2:24:10
1:13:50	1:27:30	1:45:00	2:02:30	2:20:00	2:27:41
1:15:35	1:29:35	1:47:30	2:05:25	2:23:20	2:31:12
1:17:21	1:31:40	1:50:00	2:08:20	2:26:40	2:34:43
1:19:06	1:33:45	1:52:30	2:11:15	2:30:00	2:38:14
1:20:52	1:35:50	1:55:00	2:14:10	2:33:20	2:41:45
1:22:37	1:37:55	1:57:30	2:17:05	2:36:40	2:45:16
1:24:23	1:40:00	2:00:00	2:20:00	2:40:00	2:48:47
1:26:08	1:42:05	2:02:30	2:22:55	2:43:20	2:52:18
1:27:54	1:44:10	2:05:00	2:25:50	2:46:40	2:55:49
1:29:39	1:46:15	2:07:30	2:28:45	2:50:00	2:59:20
1:31:25	1:48:20	2:10:00	2:31:40	2:53:20	3:02:51
1:33:10	1:50:25	2:12:30	2:34:35	2:56:40	3:06:22
1:34:56	1:52:30	2:15:00	2:37:30	3:00:00	3:09:53
1:36:41	1:54:35	2:17:30	2:40:25	3:03:20	3:13:24
1:38:27	1:56:40	2:20:00	2:43:20	3:06:40	3:16:55
1:40:12	1:58:45	2:22:30	2:46:15	3:10:00	3:20:26
1:41:58	2:00:50	2:25:00	2:49:10	3:13:20	3:23:57
1:43:43	2:02:55	2:27:30	2:52:05	3:16:40	3:27:28
1:45:29	2:05:00	2:30:00	2:55:00	3:20:00	3:30:59
1:47:14	2:07:05	2:32:30	2:57:55	3:23:20	3:34:29
1:49:00	2:09:10	2:35:00	3:00:50	3:26:40	3:38:00
1:50:45	2:11:15	2:37:30	3:03:45	3:30:00	3:41:31

K PACE	1 MILE	5K	10K	15K	20K
5:20	8:35	26:40	53:20	1:20:00	1:46:40
5:25	8:43	27:05	54:10	1:21:15	1:48:20
5:30	8:51	27:30	55:00	1:22:30	1:50:00
5:35	8:59	27:55	55:50	1:23:45	1:51:40
5:40	9:07	28:20	56:40	1:25:00	1:53:20
5:45	9:15	28:45	57:30	1:26:15	1:55:00
5:50	9:23	29:10	58:20	1:27:30	1:56:40
5:55	9:31	29:35	59:10	1:28:45	1:58:20
6:00	9:39	30:00	1:00:00	1:30:00	2:00:00
6:05	9:47	30:25	1:00:50	1:31:15	2:01:40
6:10	9:55	30:50	1:01:40	1:32:30	2:03:20
6:15	10:03	31:15	1:02:30	1:33:45	2:05:00
6:20	10:10	31:40	1:03:18	1:35:00	2:06:40
6:30	10:26	32:30	1:05:00	1:37:30	2:10:00
6:40	10:42	33:20	1:06:42	1:40:00	2:13:20
6:50	10:58	34:10	1:08:18	1:42:30	2:16:40
7:00	11:14	35:00	1:10:00	1:45:00	2:20:00
7:10	11:30	35:50	1:11:41	1:47:30	2:23:20
7:20	11:48	36:40	1:13:18	1:50:00	2:26:40
7:30	12:04	1:14:59	1:15:00	1:52:30	2:29:20
7:40	12:20	1:16:38	1:16:42	1:55:00	2:32:00
7:50	12:36	1:18:18	1:18:18	1:57:30	2:34:40
8:00	12:52	1:19:57	1:20:00	2:00:00	2:37:20
8:10	13:09	1:21:43	1:21:42	2:02:30	2:39:40
8:20	13:25	1:23:22	1:23:18	2:05:00	2:42:20
8:30	13:41	1:25:01	1:25:00	2:07:30	2:45:00
8:40	13:57	1:26:41	1:26:42	2:10:00	2:47:40
8:50	14:13	1:28:27	1:28:18	2:12:30	2:50:20
9:00	14:29	1:30:00	1:30:00	2:15:00	2:53:00
9:10	14:45	1:31:39	1:31:42	2:17:30	2:53:40
9:20	15:01	1:33:19	1:33:18	2:20:00	2:56:20
9:30	15:17	1:34:58	1:35:00	2:22:30	2:59:00
9:40	15:33	1:36:37	1:36:42	2:25:00	3:01:40
9:50	15:50	1:38:23	1:38:18	2:27:30	3:04:20
10:00	16:06	1:40:19	1:40:00	2:30:00	3:07:00

21.1K	25K	30K	35K	40K	42.2K
1:52:30	2:13:20	2:40:00	3:06:40	3:33:20	3:45:02
1:54:16	2:15:50	2:42:30	3:09:35	3:36:40	3:48:33
1:56:01	2:17:30	2:45:00	3:12:30	3:40:00	3:52:04
1:57:47	2:19:35	2:47:30	3:15:25	3:43:20	3:55:35
1:59:32	2:21:40	2:50:00	3:18:20	3:46:40	3:59:06
2:01:18	2:23:45	2:52:30	3:21:15	3:50:00	4:02:37
2:03:03	2:25:50	2:55:00	3:24:10	3:53:20	4:06:08
2:04:49	2:27:55	2:57:30	3:27:05	3:56:40	4:09:39
2:06:34	2:30:00	3:00:00	3:30:00	4:00:00	4:13:10
2:08:20	2:32:05	3:02:30	3:32:55	4:03:20	4:16:41
2:10:05	2:34:10	3:05:00	3:35:50	4:06:40	4:20:12
2:11:51	2:36:15	3:07:30	3:38:45	4:10:00	4:23:43
2:13:34	2:38:20	3:10:00	3:41:40	4:13:20	4:27:08
2:17:09	2:42:30	3:15:00	3:47:30	4:20:00	4:34:18
2:20:44	2:46:40	3:20:00	3:53:20	4:26:40	4:41:28
2:24:07	2:50:50	3:25:00	3:59:10	4:33:20	4:48:14
2:27:42	2:55:00	3:30:00	4:05:00	4:40:00	4:55:24
2:31:17	2:59:10	3:35:00	4:10:50	4:46:40	5:02:34
2:34:10	3:03:20	3:40:00	4:16:40	4:53:20	5:09:20
2:38:15	3:07:30	3:45:00	4:22:30	5:00:00	5:16:30
2:41:20	3:11:40	3:50:00	4:28:20	5:06:40	5:23:40
2:45:13	3:15:50	3:55:00	4:34:10	5:13:20	5:30:26
2:48:48	3:20:00	4:00:00	4:40:00	5:20:00	5:37:36
2:52:23	3:24:10	4:05:00	4:45:50	5:26:40	5:44:46
2:55:16	3:28:20	4:10:00	4:51:40	5:33:20	5:51:32
2:59:21	3:32:30	4:15:00	4:57:30	5:40:00	5:58:42
3:02:56	3:36:40	4:20:00	5:03:20	5:46:40	6:05:52
3:06:19	3:40:50	4:25:00	5:09:10	5:53:20	6:12:38
3:09:54	3:45:00	4:30:00	5:15:00	6:00:00	6:19:48
3:13:59	3:49:10	4:35:00	5:20:50	6:06:40	6:26:58
3:16:22	3:53:20	4:40:00	5:26:40	6:13:20	6:33:44
3:20:27	3:57:30	4:45:00	5:32:30	6:20:00	6:40:54
3:24:02	3:41:40	4:50:00	5:38:20	6:26:40	6:48:04
3:27:25	3:45:50	4:55:00	5:44:10	6:33:20	6:54:50
3:31:00	3:50:00	5:00:00	5:50:00	6:40:00	7:02:00

MILE PACE	5 MILES	10 MILES	13.1 MILES (Halfway)	15 MILES	20 MILES	26.2 MILES
4:45	23:45	47:30	1:02:16	1:11:15	1:35:00	2:04:33
4:50	24:10	48:20	1:03:45	1:12:30	1:36:40	2:07:44
5:00	25:00	50:00	1:05:33	1:15:00	1:40:00	2:11:06
5:10	25:50	51:40	1:06:45	1:17:30	1:43:20	2:15:28
5:15	26:15	52:30	1:08:50	1:18:45	1:45:00	2:17:40
5:20	26:40	53:20	1:10:30	1:20:00	1:46:50	2:19:50
5:30	27:30	55:00	1:12:08	1:22:30	1:50:00	2:24:12
5:40	28:20	56:40	1:13:30	1:25:00	1:53:20	2:28:20
5:45	28:45	57:30	1:15:23	1:26:15	1:55:00	2:30:46
5:50	29:10	58:20	1:16:45	1:27:30	1:56:40	2:32:56
6:00	30:00	1:00:00	1:18:39	1:30:00	2:00:00	2:37:19
6:10	30:50	1:01:40	1:20:23	1:32:30	2:03:20	2:41:41
6:15	31:15	1:02:30	1:21:56	1:33:45	2:05:00	2:43:53
6:20	31:40	1:03:20	1:23:10	1:35:00	2:06:40	2:46:03
6:30	32:30	1:05:00	1:25:13	1:37:30	2:10:00	2:50:25
6:40	33:20	1:06:40	1:26:30	1:40:00	2:13:20	2:54:47
6:45	33:45	1:07:30	1:28:29	1:41:15	2:15:00	2:56:59
6:50	34:10	1:08:20	1:29:15	1:42:30	2:16:40	2:59:09
7:00	35:00	1:10:00	1:31:46	1:45:00	2:20:00	3:03:33
7:10	35:50	1:11:40	1:33:14	1:47:30	2:23:20	3:07:55
7:15	36:15	1:12:30	1:35:03	1:48:45	2:25:00	3:10:06
7:20	36:40	1:13:20	1:36:10	1:50:00	2:26:40	3:12:17
7:30	37:30	1:15:00	1:38:19	1:52:30	2:30:00	3:16:39
7:40	38:20	1:16:40	1:40:10	1:55:00	2:33:20	3:21:01
7:45	38:45	1:17:30	1:41:36	1:56:15	2:35:00	3:23:13
7:50	39:10	1:18:20	1:42:46	1:57:30	2:36:40	3:25:23
8:00	40:00	1:20:00	1:44:53	2:00:00	2:40:00	3:29:45
8:10	40:50	1:21:40	1:46:40	2:02:30	2:43:20	3:34:07
8:15	41:15	1:22;30	1:48:10	2:03:45	2:45:00	3:36:20
8:20	41:40	1:23:20	1:49:13	2:05:00	2:46:40	3:38:29
8:30	42:30	1:25:00	1:51:26	2:07:30	2:50:00	3:42:51
8:40	43:20	1:26:40	1:53:10	2:10:00	2:53:20	3:47:13
8:45	43:45	1:27:30	1:54:43	2:11:15	2:55:00	3:49:26

MILE PACE	5 MILES	10 MILES	13.1 MILES (Halfway)	15 MILES	20 MILES	26.2 MILES
8:50	44:10	1:28:20	1:56:10	2:12:30	2:56:40	3:51:35
9:00	45:00	1:30:00	1:57:59	2:15:00	3:00:00	3:56:00
9:10	45:50	1:31:40	1:59:10	2:17:30	3:03:20	4:00:22
9:15	46:15	1:32:30	2:01:16	2:18:45	3:05:00	4:02:32
9:20	46:40	1:33:20	2:02:10	2:20:00	3:06:40	4:04:44
9:30	47:30	1:35:00	2:04:33	2:22:30	3:10:00	2:09:06
9:40	48:20	1:36:40	2:05:47	2:25:00	3:13:20	4:13:28
9:45	48:45	1:37:30	2:07:49	2:26:15	3:15:00	4:15:33
9:50	49:10	1:38:20	2:09:10	2:27:30	3:16:40	4:17:50
10:00	50:00	1:40:00	2:11:06	2:30:00	3:20:00	4:22:13
10:10	50:50	1:41:40	2:13:04	2:32:30	3:23:20	4:26:33
10:20	51:40	1:43:20	2:15:28	2:35:00	3:26:40	4:30:56
10:30	52:30	1:45:00	2:17:39	2:37:30	3:30:00	4:35:18
10:40	53:20	1:46:40	2:19:50	2:40:00	3:33:20	4:39:40
10:50	54:10	1:48:20	2:22:01	2:42:30	3:36:40	4:44:02
11:00	55:00	1:50:00	2:24:12	2:45:00	3:40:00	4:48:24
11:10	55:50	1:51:40	2:26:23	2:47:30	3:43:20	4:52:47
11:20	56:40	1:53:20	2:28:34	2:50:00	3:46:40	4:57:09
11:30	57:30	1:55:00	2:30:45	2:52:30	3:50:00	5:01:31
11:40	58:20	1:56:40	2:32:57	2:55:00	3:53:20	5:05:53
11:50	59:10	1:58:20	2:35:08	2:57:30	3:56:40	5:10:15
12:00	1:00:00	2:00:00	2:37:19	3:00:00	4:00:00	5:14:37
12:10	1:00:50	2:01:40	2:39:30	3:02:30	4:03:20	5:19:00
12:20	1:01:40	2:03:20	2:41:41	3:05:00	4:06:40	5:23:22
12:30	1:02:30	2:05:00	2:43:52	3:07:30	4:10:00	5:27:44
12:40	1:03:20	2:06:40	2:46:03	3:10:00	4:13:20	5:32:06
12:50	1:04:10	2:08:20	2:48:14	3:12:30	4:16:40	5:36:28
13:00	1:05:00	2:10:00	2:50:25	3:15:00	4:20:00	5:40:51
13:10	1:05:50	2:11:40	2:52:36	3:17:30	4:23:20	5:45:13
13:20	1:06:40	2:13:20	2:54:48	3:20:00	4:26:40	5:49:35
13:30	1:07:30	2:15:00	2:56:59	3:22:30	4:30:00	5:53:57
13:40	1:08:20	2:16:40	2:59:10	3:25:00	4:33:20	5:58:19
13:50	1:09:10	2:18:20	3:01:21	3:27:30	4:36:40	6:02:42

MILE PACE	5 MILES	10 MILES	13.1 MILES (Halfway)	15 MILES	20 MILES	26.2 MILES
14:00	1:10:00	2:20:00	3:03:32	3:30:00	4:40:00	6:07:04
14:10	1:10:50	2:21:40	3:05:43	3:32:30	4:43:20	6:11:26
14:20	1:11:40	2:23:20	3:07:54	3:35:00	4:46:40	6:15:48
14:30	1:12:30	2:25:00	3:10:05	3:37:30	4:50:00	6:20:10
14:40	1:13:20	2:26:40	3:12:16	3:40:00	4:53:20	6:24:32
14:50	1:14:10	2:28:20	3:14:27	3:42:30	4:56:40	6:28:55
15:00	1:15:00	2:30:00	3:16:38	3:45:00	5:00:00	6:33:17

Works Cited

Chapter 1

Buccola, VA, and WJ Stone. "Effects of jogging and cycling programmes on physiological and personality variables in middle aged men." *Research Quarterly* 46 (1975): 134-139.

Eide, R. "The relationship between body image, self-image and physical activity." *Scandinavian Journal of Social Medicine* 29 (1982, suppl.): 109-112.

Hartung, GH, and EJ Farge. "Personality and physiological traits in middle-aged runners and joggers." *Journal of Gerontology* 32 (1977): 541-548.

Mahle Lutter, Judy, and Lynn Jaffee. *The Bodywise Woman.* Champaign, Illinois: Human Kinetics, 1996.

McPherson, BD, A Paivio, MS Yuhasz, PA Rechnitzer, HA Pickard, and NM Lefcoe. "Psychological effects of an exercise program for post-infarct and normal adult men." *Journal of Sports Medicine and Physical Fitness* 7 (2) (1967): 95-102.

Noakes, Tim, MD. *Lore of Running.* Champaign, Illinois: Leisure Press, 1991.

Sharp, MW, and RR Reilley. "The relationship of aerobic physical fitness to selected personality traits." *Journal of Clinical Psychology* 31 (1975): 428-430.

Wilson, VE, NC Morley, and EI Bird. "Mood profiles in marathon runners, joggers and non-exercisers." *Perceptual and Motor Skills* 50 (1980): 117-118.

Young, RJ, and AH Ismail. "The personality differences of adult men before and after a physical fitness program." *Research Quarterly* (1976).

Young, RJ, and AH Ismail. "Relationships between anthropometric, physiological, biochemical and personality variables before and after a four month conditioning program for middle-aged men." *Journal of Sports Medicine and Physical Fitness* 16: 267-276.

Young, RJ, and AH Ismail. "Comparison of selected physiological and personality variables in regular and non-regular adult male exercisers." *Research Quarterly* 48 (1997): 617-622.

ADDITIONAL SOURCES

National Survey of Women's Health, 1993. Conducted by the Commonwealth Fund, by Louis Harris and Associates, U.S.

National Women's Health Information Center, United States Department of Health and Human Services.

Chapter 2

Bahrke, MS, and WP Morgan. "Anxiety reduction following exercise and meditation." *The Psychology of Running.* MH Sacks and ML Sachs (eds.). Champaign, Illinois: Human Kinetics, 1981.

Blumenthal, JA, RS Williams, TL Needles, and AG Wallace. "Psychological changes accompany aerobic exercise in healthy middle-aged adults." *Psychosomatic Medicine* 44 (1982): 529-553.

De Vries, HA. "Tranquilizer effect of exercise: A critical review." *The Physician and Sportsmedicine* 9 (Nov 1981): 47-55.

Dienstbier, RA, Crabbe, GO Johnson, W Thorland, JA Jorgensen, MM Sader, and DC Lavelle. "Exercise and stress tolerance." *Psychology of Running*. MH Sacks and ML Sachs (eds.). Champaign, Illinois: Human Kinetics, 1981.

Guyot, GW, L Fairchild, and J Nickens. "Death concerns of runners and non-runners." *Journal of Sports Medicine and Physical Fitness* 24 (1984): 139-143.

Howard, JH, DA Cunningham, and PA Rechnitzer. "Physical activity as a moderator of life events and somatic complaints: A longitudinal study." *Canadian Journal of Applied Sport Science* 9 (1984): 194-200.

Johnsgard, Keith W, Ph.D. *The Exercise Prescription for Depression and Anxiety.* New York: Plenum Press, 1989.

Nuori, S, and J Beer. "Relations of moderate physical activity to scores on hostility, aggression and trait-anxiety." *Perceptive and Motor Skills* 68 (1989): 1191-1194.

Salmon, P. "Effects of physical exercise on anxiety, depression and sensitivity to stress: A unifying theory." Department of Clinical Psychology, University of Liverpool, UK. *Clinical Psychology Review* 21 (1) (Feb 2001): 33-61.

Stephens, T. "Physical activity and mental health in the United States and Canada: Evidence from four population surveys." *Preventative Medicine* 17 (1988): 35-47.

Topp, R. "Effect of relaxation or exercise on undergraduates' test anxiety." *Perceptive and Motor Skills* 69 (1989): 35-41.

ADDITIONAL SOURCES

Healthy People 2000, U.S. Dept of Health and Human Services.

National Health Interview Study, 1995: Year 2000 Objectives Supplement. U.S. Department of Health and Human Services, National Center for Health Statistics.

National Institute for Occupational Safety and Health and the American Psychological Association, March 1999, Fourth Annual Conference.

Chapter 3

Carter, R. "Exercise and happiness." *Journal of Sports Medicine* 17 (1977): 307-313.

Dimeo, F, M Bauer, I Varahram, G Proest, and U Halter. Department of Sports Medicine, Freie University, Berlin. Department of Psychiatry. "Benefits from aerobic exercise in patients with major depression: A pilot study." *British Journal of Sports Medicine* 35 (2) (Apr 2001): 114-117.

Farmer, ME, BZ Locke, EK Mo'sciski, AL Dannenberg, DB Larson, and LS Radloff. "Physical activity and depressive symptoms: The NHANES I epidemiologic follow-up study." *American Journal of Epidemiology* 128 (1988): 1340-1351.

Jaffee, Lynn. "Health benefits, concerns and practices of Melpomene members." *The Melpomene Journal* 19 (2) (summer 2000): 26-30.

Johnsgard, Keith W, Ph.D. *The Exercise Prescription for Depression and Anxiety.* New York: Plenum Press, 1989.
McCann, IL, and DS Holmes. "Influence of aerobic exercise on depression." *Journal of Personal and Social Psychology* 46 (1984): 1142-1147.
Paluska, SA, and TL Schwenk. "Physical activity and mental health: Current concepts." *Journal of Sports Medicine* 29 (3) (Mar 2000): 167-180.
Ross, DL, and DS Hayes. "Exercise and psychologic well-being in the community." *American Journal of Epidemiology* 127 (1988): 762-771.
Roth, DL, and DS Holmes. "Influence of aerobic exercise training and relaxation training on physical and psychologic health following stressful life events." *Psychosomatic Medicine* 49 (1987): 355-365.

ADDITIONAL SOURCES

Canadian Centre for Addiction and Mental Health.
The U.S. National Institute of Mental Health.

Chapter 4

Aganoff, JA, and GJ Boyle. Department of Psychology, University of Queensland, Australia. "Aerobic exercise, mood states and menstrual cycle symptoms." *Journal of Psychosomatic Research* 38 (3) (Apr 1994): 183-192.
Choi, PY, and P Salmon. Department of Psychology, University of Nottingham, UK. "Symptom changes across the menstrual cycle in competitive sportswomen, exercisers and sedentary women." *British Journal of Clinical Psychology* 34 (3) (Sept 1995): 447-460.
Kowalchik, Claire. *The Complete Book of Running for Women.* New York: Pocket Books, 1999.
Mahle Lutter, Judy, and Lynn Jaffee. *The Bodywise Woman.* Champaign, Illinois: Human Kinetics, 1996.
Mahle Lutter, Judy, and Lynn Jaffee, "Changes in running associated with menopause and aging. A preliminary investigation." June 1998 Melpomene and Runner's World Questionnaire. *Melpomene Journal* (spring 1999): 19.
Miszko, TA, and ME Cress. Department of Exercise Science, University of Georgia. "A lifetime of fitness: Exercise in the perimenopausal and postmenopausal woman." *Clinics in Sports Medicine* 19 (2) (Apr 2000): 215-232.
Prior, JC, Y Vigna, and N Alojada. "Conditioning exercise decreases premenstrual symptoms: A prospective controlled three-month trial." *The European Journal of Applied Physiology and Occupational Physiology* 55 (4) (1986): 349-355.

ADDITIONAL SOURCES

American Journal of Public Health 90 (Jan 2000): 134-138.
Project AWARE (Association of Women for the Advancement of Research and Education).
Report presented by the Consensus Conference form the National Institutes of Health, NIH Consensus Development Panel on Osteoporosis Prevention, Diagnosis and Therapy, published in the *Journal of American Medical Association.*

Chapter 5

Jaffee, Lynn, and Linda Feltes. "Factors affecting women's motivation for physical activity." Melpomene Institute 1996 Self Magazine Questionnaire. *Melpomene Journal* (fall 1997).

Chapter 6

Kowalchik, Claire. *The Complete Book of Running for Women.* New York: Pocket Books, 1999.

Chapter 10

Ray, US, S Mukhopadhyaya, S Purkayasthas, U Asnani, OS Tomer, R Prashad, L Thakur, and W Selvamurthy. Defence Institute of Physiology and Allied Sciences, Luknow Road, Delhi. "Effect of yogic exercise on physical and mental health of young fellowship course trainees." *Indian Journal of Physiology and Pharmacology* 45 (1) (Jan 2001): 37-53.

Chapter 11

Body Mass Index, American Dietetic Association.

Report of the Dietary Guidelines Committee on the Dietary Guidelines for Americans, 1995.

Chapter 14

Baekeland, F. "Exercise deprivation: Sleep and psychological reactions." *Archives of General Psychiatry* 22 (1970): 365-369.

Callen, KE. "Mental and emotional aspects of long-distance running." *Psychosomatics* 24 (1983): 133-151.

Sacks, MH. "Running addiction: A clinical report." *Psychology of Running*. MH Sacks and ML Sachs (eds.). Champaign, Illinois: Human Kinetics, 1981.

Wildmann, J, A Krugar, M Schmole, J Niemann, and H Matthaei. "Increase of circulatory beta-endorphine-like immunoreactivity correlates with the change in feeling of pleasantness after running." *Life Sciences* 38 (1986): 997-1003.

Chapter 17

Clapp, James F, III. Department of Reproductive Biology, Case Western Reserve University School of Medicine, Cleveland, Ohio."Exercise during pregnancy: A clinical update." *Clinics in Sports Medicine* 19 (2) (Apr 2000): 273-286.

Clapp, James F, III. *Exercising Through Your Pregnancy*. Champaign, Illinois: Human Kinetics, 1998.

Clapp, James F, III. "Exercise in pregnancy: A brief clinical review." *Fetal Medicine Review* 2 (1990): 99-101.

Goodwin, A, J Astbury, and J McMeekan. University of Melbourne, Victoria, Australia. "Body image and psychological well-being in pregnancy: A comparison of exercisers and non-exercisers." *Australian and New Zealand Journal of Obstetrics and Gynaecology* 40 (4) (Nov 2000): 442-447.

Spinelli, Margaret G, MD. "Antepartum and post-partum depression." *The Journal of Gender-Specific Medicine* 1 (2) (1998): 33-36.

ADDITIONAL SOURCES

The American College of Obstetricians and Gynecologists Technical Bulletin 189. "Exercising during pregnancy and the post-partum period." Washington, D.C., 1994.

Index